Effective Writing

A Handbook with Stories for Lawyers

Effective Writing

A Handbook with Stories for Lawyers

John Phelps Warnock, J.D, M.A. (Oxon)
with Harold C. Warnock, LL.B.

Parlor Press
West Lafayette, Indiana
www.parlorpress.com

Parlor Press LLC, West Lafayette, Indiana 47906

SAN: 254-8879

Library of Congress Control Number: 2003101596

Effective Writing: A Handbook with Stories for Lawyers
  by John Phelps Warnock, with Harold C. Warnock
Includes index.
Contents: Introduction – Writing through the day – Writing through
  the trial – Writing through the appeal – Writing for the future :
  contracts and wills and trusts – Rewrite for effectiveness – Checklist
  inventory – Index of topics
1. Warnock, John Phelps 1941— . 2. Warnock, Harold C. 1912
  — 1997. 3. Legal composition. 4. Law—United States—language.
  5. Law—United States—methodology. 6. Rhetoric.
I. Title

ISBN 0-9724772-7-6 (Paper)
ISBN 0-9724772-4-1 (Cloth)
ISBN 0-9724772-6-8 (Adobe Acrobat eBook)

Parlor Press, LLC is an independent publisher of scholarly and trade titles
in print and multimedia formats. This book is also available in cloth, as
well as in Adobe Acrobat eBook Reader and Night Kitchen (TK3) formats, from Parlor Press on the WWW at http://www.parlorpress.com.
For submission information or to find out about Parlor Press publications, write to Parlor Press, 816 Robinson St., West Lafayette, Indiana,
47906, or e-mail editor@parlorpress.com.

Dedication

Hal Warnock, 1912-1997
Honest Lawyer One Flight Up

General Table of Contents

Acknowledgments xv

1 Introduction 1

2 Writing through the Day 21

3 Writing through the Trial 51

4 Writing through the Appeal   78

5 Writing for the Future: Contracts and Wills and Trusts   96

6 Rewrite for Effectiveness   121

Checklist Inventory   176
Index of Topics   179

Detailed Table of Contents

3

4

Writing through the Appeal   78

5

Acknowledgments

Lawyers work in a world where it is hard to presume that any one person or set of beliefs has a corner on the truth. Maybe that is why they tend to be good people and good company. Not everyone would agree with this proposition about lawyers, but it reflects my experience, and I want to thank the many lawyers and judges who over the years have been good people, good company, in my life.

Lawyers also tend to tell a good story. While I was working on this book, many of them shared their stories about writing with me. These stories brought the world of legal writing alive, and I decided they belonged in this book in some form. I want to thank them all. I hope their spirit abides in the "sidebars" that appear in this book.

I want to thank my father, a lawyer for almost sixty years, with whom I worked in the last stages of his life on the first stages of this book. The evidence is that my father was a very good lawyer indeed. I also know that he cared deeply about the practice of law, about language, about writing, and about teaching new lawyers about these things. I hope this book advances his project.

For an important early lesson in the difference between effective and good writing, I would like to thank the Assistant Attorney General in the Department of Justice who was my boss in the summer during law school that I was an intern in the Administrative Division. One day that summer while I was working with a form, I realized I could improve it substantially. I re-drafted it and took it to my boss. He allowed that I had improved it. "So what do I do now?" I asked. "Take it downstairs to the guy in charge of forms," he said, "and make it seem to be his idea."

For a writing assignment from which I may have learned more and more quickly than any other, I want to thank the late Richard Chambers, Chief Judge of the U.S. Court of Appeals for the Ninth Circuit for many years. When I began work as his clerk he informed me that the bench memos I was to prepare for him before oral argument were to be no longer than three octavo-sized pages, that is to say, a page-and-a-half long. This rule applied even if the file that had come up on appeal was four feet thick and the briefs fifty pages long. I found it was possible to do this much more often than I would have thought. I learned a lot from this about how to make sentences count.

Thanks to three friends over many years all of whom were very good lawyers and then very good judges and who read chapters of the manuscript and offered advice and stories, the late Richard Bilby (U.S. District Court), Mike Lacagnina, (Arizona Court of Appeals) and the late Bill Tinny (Superior Court of Pima County). Of the many practicing lawyers who have helped me with the book, I want to thank particularly Tom Chandler, Steve Corradini, Robert Fleming, Sam Hatcher, Terry Jackson, Bob Lesher, Mick Rusing, Tom Slutes, Nicole Smithson, Steve Thomas, Gordon Waterfall. Bob Feldman was especially generous with stories. Special thanks are due to Phil Hall, partner in the firm of Miller, Pitt & McAnally, and to the other lawyers in that firm who at Phil's invitation read a version of the manuscript and added a meeting with me to their busy schedules: Tom Kotter, Gerald Malz, Grace McIlvain, Armando Rivera, Carol Summers, and Jan Wezelman. I want to thank the Honorable M. Blane Michael of the U. S. Court of Appeals for the Fourth Circuit and more importantly my roommate in law school for offering such a shining example of what it is to be good people, good company.

I want to thank Professor Dwight Stevenson of the University of Michigan who twenty-or-so years ago invited me to present the first workshop on writing I offered to state court judges. I want to thank Harold Kolb of the University of Virginia who invited me soon after that to work at the first Judgment Writing Seminar offered to Canadian judges through the Canadian Institute for the Administration of Justice. This summer workshop has been offered by CIAJ for over twenty years now and is now considered one of CIAJ's most successful educational programs. I want to thank the many judges I've worked with in the Seminar who have been my students and teachers. I want to thank also the other members of the faculty for the Seminar, who taught me too, and who, like the judges who came to work on their writing, were also good people, good company: Phil Beidler, Ed Berry, Peter Buitenhaus, George Byrnes, the Honorable Adelle Fruman, Greig Henderson, the Honorable Nicole Duval Hesler, Judith Herz, the Honorable John Laskin, Jay Ludwig, Jim Raymond, the Honorable Bill Stevenson, and the presiding lights during this time, the Honorable James Carnwath, the Honorable Louise Mailhot, and Christine Huglot-Robertson.

Thanks to Professors Charles Ares, Kay Kavanagh, and Winton Woods of the University of Arizona's College of Law for helpful consultations and encouragement. Thanks to Dottie Larson and Michael Moore for consultations on design.

I want to thank Walter Eggers III, now with Holland & Hart in Cheyenne, Wyoming who I have watched become a fine lawyer and writer and who offered several stories and excellent suggestions over the years I worked on this book. Thanks also to Jane Eggers, Director of the Citizens Jury Project for the Fund for Modern Courts, who has always been able to see what matters in writing and other art.

For their sustained and imaginative efforts to develop a view of writing more adequate to the task, I want to thank my colleagues in the new (and old) discipline of Rhetoric and Composition that has taken shape in college English Departments over the last thirty-or-so years. I want to thank Ed White for reading and responding in his clear, definite, and perspicuous way to one of the chapters.

David Blakesley of Parlor Press has been a wonderfully encouraging and skillful editor.

Tilly, you are woven into the fabric of it all.

1 Introduction

The Authors

The authors of this book are an English professor who has a law degree and has worked for over twenty years with judges and lawyers on writing, and a respected lawyer who in fifty-nine years of practice learned a lot about effective writing.

The English professor, John Phelps Warnock, has a J.D. from the New York University School of Law, where he was a Root-Tilden Scholar. In 1967, he worked as an intern in the United States Department of Justice. From 1968 to 1969, he was the law clerk for Chief Judge Richard Chambers of the United States Court of Appeals for the Ninth Circuit. He is a member of the Arizona Bar. Over the last twenty-five years, he has consulted on legal writing to law firms and judicial groups in the United States and for most of that time has been a member of the faculty for the Judgment Writing Seminar offered by the Canadian Institute for the Administration of Justice. He is a graduate of Amherst College, where he was a Sloan scholar, and Oxford University, where he was a Keasbey scholar. He now teaches at the University of Arizona where his fields of specialization are rhetoric, composition, literary nonfiction, and the teaching of English.

The lawyer, Harold C. "Hal" Warnock (1912-1997), was a member of the Arizona Bar for over sixty years. He was a Fellow of the American College of Trial Lawyers and a Fellow of the American College of Trust and Estate Counsel. He appeared in Los Angeles, San Francisco, New York,

Washington, D.C., and in many smaller cities, usually on behalf of target defendants. He was a founding member of the Arizona Chapter of the American Board of Trial Advocates and served as President of the National Association of Railroad Trial Counsel. He was twice appointed by the governor of the state as Co-Chair of the Arizona Commission on Uniform Laws, and was appointed in 1991 as Arizona contact person for the Joint Editorial Board of the Uniform Probate Code Commission. Besides the writing he did as a practicing lawyer, he published articles about the law and nonfiction about his experiences playing baseball for the St. Louis Browns in the 1930s.

Statement of the Case

This book will be useful to any lawyer, new or experienced, who wants to write more effectively. It may be of special value to lawyers embarking on the practice of law who are realizing what they didn't learn in law school. It will also be useful to paralegals, legal assistants, and law clerks.

This book differs from other books about legal writing in

- its primary focus on *effective* (as opposed to *good*) legal writing,

- its attention to how writing contributes to thinking for lawyers,

- its emphasis on *rewriting* and how to do it effectively,

- its treatment of *legal style* in terms of what it contributes to *effective* legal writing,

- its address to some of the important kinds of *informal writing* that lawyers do (like letters and writing to support oral argument), and

- its consideration of *electronic technologies* and effective writing.

We will refer to some statutes, rules, and cases but offer few citations and no footnotes. This book is not a work of legal scholarship. In the section "Writing through the Trial," we rely on the Federal Rules of Civil Procedure. Most courts in the United States follow them or rules adopted from them. In the chapter "Writing through the Appeal," we rely on the Federal Rules of Appellate Procedure.

To make the principles and practices of legal writing more real to readers, the book offers "sidebars" throughout—brief comments and stories by judges, practicing lawyers, writers, and teachers of writing that throw some light on the matters being considered at that moment.

Effective (rather than *good*) legal writing is the goal here. *Good* writing is correct, clear, and sometimes graceful and elegant. We believe deeply in the value of *good* writing. But books about legal writing tend to assume *good* writing is necessarily what will be *good for* any situation. That's not quite right, especially for lawyers.

We realize this last claim might be controversial, though we imagine most lawyers at least suspect that it's true. We will take a moment here, then, to argue the point.

In school, students who do well as writers know that what will count as *good* writing is what is *good for* the particular class and teacher. This may seem to them a disappointing, even a scandalous state of affairs. Students may feel—and their teachers may also—that if all were as it should be, *good* writing would be all that is needed to thrive in any situation. The more successful students know better than to assume that it is. The writing that is good for school—sometimes called "academic writing"—is the writing that is good for the particular taskmasters and tasks of the particular school situation.

In law school, the students who do well realize that *good* writing is what is *good for* law school examinations of the sort given by a particular professor. Professors in law schools work in their various ways to teach law students important principles in particular areas of the law and more generally—it is often said—how to *think* like a lawyer. It is apparent that law students can learn how to think like a lawyer without, unfortunately, learning how to write effectively in the practice of law. One problem law students have is that the examinations typically given in law school classes do not offer good models of effective legal writing. In these examinations, it is not uncommon for students to be rewarded in proportion to the number of issues they can identify in a given fact situation. Practicing lawyers need to be able to recognize issues, needless to say, but they also need to select the important ones for their particular situation and readers, and give those issues the right emphasis. Another problem law students face is that the opinions analyzed in law school are never addressed in terms of their effectiveness as writing. Many opinions, including many of those in the casebooks, are very badly written. Law students might well come to assume that that is what legal writing is supposed to be like.

In the law school course that is said to teach legal writing, students learn the conventions of citation and techniques of legal research typically by writing an in-house memorandum and a brief on appeal. In these one- or two-unit courses, little time is available for considering what makes such documents effective, beyond correctness in the conventions of citation and what may be called "logical" development of the argument. Law students certainly need to learn the conventions of research and correctness and how to research the law. But if they infer from the Legal Research and Writing courses that in the practice of law they will be writing mostly memoranda and briefs on appeal, they will have to do some unlearning before they will be able to write effectively as practicing lawyers.

> On my first day on the job, Judge Chambers introduced me to two Circuit Court colleagues on the elevator. "This is my new law clerk. He's been in school for the last 22 years. He's got a lot of un-learning to do."

What about writing for the law review? While such writing can prepare a student for work as a legal scholar, whose job it is to explore issues, it is not a good model for practicing lawyers, whose job it is to argue cases for clients (among other things), or even for appellate court judges, whose job it is to decide cases. We do see a lot of law-review-like writing in appellate opinions, perhaps because most law clerks in appellate courts have just served on law reviews.

Effective legal writing is what is good for the practice of law, for the varied purposes and readers that practicing lawyers have. In the practice of law, what is "good" in one situation may not be "good" in another. Moreover, what is "good for" the task at hand may not even be "good" writing, as will appear.

In placing the emphasis on *effective* writing, we do not mean to imply that law students and lawyers needn't concern themselves with learning how to produce correct, clear, coherent, "logical" prose. We mean only to say that when effectiveness is the criterion, there's more to think about than that.

Still less do we mean to imply approval of the shabby ethical conduct that the public too often takes to be a hallmark of the legal profession. We will not encourage writing that deceives, baffles, or intimidates its readers. Even "good" writing can do this: *effective* writing almost never does. Writing that is *intended* to deceive, or baffle, or intimidate is short-sighted. It tends to backfire. The better lawyers know this. They know that to write effectively is also to meet the highest standards of professionalism and ethics.

Effective writing does not guarantee success. In the practice of law, outcomes are uncertain. No lawyer likes to lose, but every lawyer will sometimes, no matter how effective his or her own writing or how ineffective the other side's. People who can't stand uncertainty and can't bounce back after a defeat should probably consider another line of work.

Why work at writing effectively then?

- Effective writing isn't what wins every time: it's what gives you your best chance of winning. If you work at writing effectively, you will lose less often.

- When you do lose, at least it won't be because you weren't able to do what lawyers are supposed to be able to do—write effectively.

- In the situations in the practice of law where there are no clear winners and losers, writing effectively will help you achieve the best result all around, for your client and for yourself.

- Effective writing will improve your standing with your peers, which is important to effectiveness and success in the long term.

Young delinquent to Homer Simpson on TV: "That's it. I don't believe in anything anymore. I'm going to go to law school!"

Conclusion of an unreported appellate decision: "We reverse for the numerous errors of fact and law. It's a shame though. The brief was so well-written."

To become more effective, writers cannot rely only on learning rules of writing style. They must begin to cultivate certain habits of mind and writing practice that are essential to learning to write more effectively. We begin by setting out some of these habits of mind and writing practice. We go on to deal specifically with many of the different kinds of writing lawyers do:

> *Writing through the Day* deals with three crucial aspects of writing in the practice of law that are not usually addressed in law school: facts, forms, and letters.

> *Writing through the Trial* addresses the kinds of writing lawyers do while litigating in the order in which they do them.

> *Writing through the Appeal* does the same thing for appeals.

> *Writing for the Future* addresses principles of effective writing for contracts and wills and trusts.

> *Rewrite for Effectiveness*, the final chapter, sets out principles of *rewriting*, including editing for style. Learning to *rewrite* effectively is absolutely essential to learning to write effectively.

Prepare to Write Effectively: Habits of Mind and Practice

Checklist: Habits of Mind and Practice

- Notice effective writing.
- Get help from others on your writing.
- Recognize that writing is a powerful tool for thinking.
- Understand the importance of planning.
- Notice that legal writing, like other writing, has voice and communicates attitudes toward the reader.
- Understand that revision is crucial.

If legal writers want to write more effectively, they will have to do more than read someone's book or attend a seminar and learn the principles enunciated there. They will have to cultivate habits of mind and writing practice that lead to more effective writing. The process begins when we become aware of how important these habits are, and it continues in daily practice.

Notice Effective Writing

No book, ours included, will make much difference to a writer who doesn't appreciate the difference effective writing can make. Ineffective writers can be the last to appreciate the difference it makes, unfortunately.

Until we start to care about becoming more effective as writers, we probably won't notice writing that is effective. Most readers—even if they are ineffective writers—do notice when writing is simply *bad*. We notice it but don't dwell on it: none of us gives any more time than absolutely necessary to writing that is ineffective. Those who want to become more effective writers pay attention to the stuff that works and pause to consider what makes it work.

In the practice of law, effective writing does not call attention to itself as writing. Writing that calls attention to itself is likely to distract the reader. Effective legal argument makes what it is arguing seem right, not stylish. Such writing can seem ordinary and easy to produce, but it's not. In your search for effective writing, you should pay special attention to the writing that achieves this apparent ease and transparency.

Begin now to cultivate the habit of noticing writing that seems particularly effective. Notice it wherever you find it—in newspapers, letters you receive, books you read, office memos, judicial opinions. Take a moment to ask how this writing achieves its effects. You may not always be able to say exactly how. But over time, this habit of attention will help you write more effectively yourself.

Get Help from Others on Your Writing

Effective writers get help from others on their writing. We picture the ideal writer hunched over the desk, brow furrowed, locked in solitary struggle with language. And so sometimes we are. But effective writers know they are writing to be read, and they know how difficult it is to produce

> What I'm struck by more often is lawyers who are supposed to be pretty good who aren't very good writers. How do they do that, I wonder?
>
> —An A-rated lawyer

writing that will be read as the writer would wish it to be read. Before they release their work to their intended readers, they find other readers and writers to help them revise.

They seek listeners too. Reading aloud to another is a wonderfully instructive experience for writers. This "other" need not be an expert: we often learn more about the effectiveness of the *writing* from reading to an audience that can't be expected to fill in the blanks for us.

Even reading aloud to ourselves can help us see how to improve our drafts. We read aloud more slowly than we do when we read silently. Slowing down helps us see and hear more clearly what our language is doing. Reading aloud also allows us to *experience* our language. When we find ourselves saying "blah-blah-blah" when we pass through a passage in our drafts, or when we find ourselves hurrying through, or stumbling, we are experiencing the writing as a reader would. When writers read their material aloud with the aim of making it better, they *always* see a way to make it better.

A *good* reader or listener is a priceless asset for a writer. Not everyone is willing to take the time, and not everyone who takes the time is able to respond in ways that help the writer see how to make the writing more effective. Nevertheless, *all the effective writers we know seek readers and find them.*

Recognize That Writing Is a Powerful Tool for Thinking

Many respected professional writers have testified to the way writing helps them think:

> I always write a thing first and think about it afterward, which is not a bad procedure, because the easiest way to have consecutive thoughts is to start putting them down.
>
> —E. B. White

> Most often I come to an understanding of what I am writing about as I write it.
>
> —C. Day Lewis

I was working on a draft with my boss not long after I joined the firm. My boss had worked me and my draft over for the third time when he finally said, "Okay, let's see what Ralph thinks." Ralph was the old partner who had hired my boss. We went down to the old man's office. He read it, then looked up. 'We don't really need this paragraph, now do we?' he said. I had to grin when I saw that happen to my boss, but I learned something important there.

—An associate

> *I write to find out what I am thinking about.*
>
> —Edward Albee

For legal writers too, writing is a powerful tool for thinking and not just a vehicle for pre-existing thoughts. Like thinking, writing can take us in directions we hadn't expected when we sat down to write. Thought emerges and is clarified through writing and rewriting. Writing *out* thoughts allows rethinking—revision—of a sort that would be difficult or impossible without having written.

Once we notice this feature of writing, we learn not to postpone writing until our thoughts have become completely clear, and we learn not to terminate our thinking prematurely, just because we've written something down or dictated something that has been transcribed for us. Writing can *impede* thought—if it is taken as only a means of communicating thought rather than as a means for thinking in the first place. Once we understand that writing is thinking, we stop being disappointed when our writing surprises us and takes us in a new direction.

When we understand that writing is a means of thinking, we can learn to use it for more effective *and* more efficient thinking and revision. Thinking is not easy or neat much of the time. It can be unsettling to face up to the actualities of thinking and writing, just as it can be unsettling to face up to the actualities of legislation and food preparation. Still, if we want to write effectively, we need to face up to those actualities and learn how to deal with them.

Understand the Importance of Planning

A crucial part of the writing process is the part that happens *before* any draft is produced. Notes from client interviews, tentative statements of the issue, outlines, dictated summaries of conversations or days in court—all are part of the writing process and can be resources for writers. All can help with the thinking and planning that should *precede* drafting.

Planning is crucial to effective, and efficient, drafting. Time is a precious resource for lawyers, and they must be concerned with efficiency, as well as effectiveness. Efficient

The British essayist Charles Lamb said he was so horrified by the messiness of the manuscript of Milton's *Lycidas* that he resolved never to go into an artist's workshop again.

drafting and revising is that which takes no more time than is necessary to produce effective writing. When writing is allowed to function as the powerful tool for thinking that it can be, it does not always proceed in neat and orderly ways. To be effective for a reader, the writing that is thinking will almost always have to be revised to meet the requirements of the reader. Planning is crucial to get from the thinking a lawyer needs to do to the *results* of thinking that a reader needs to see.

Writing promotes planning, as it does thinking. Having a good plan means having more than having a vague sense of some form to follow. It means having a clear sense of what you want the writing to DO, for whom, and how. One study of professional writers showed them spending over 60% of their writing time in planning and thinking by means of writing that *preceded* drafting.

Lawyers procrastinate about writing, as all writers do. But when writers understand how writing promotes thinking and how important the writing that precedes drafting can be, they can learn to procrastinate less. They can stop postponing their writing in the hope that some fine day they will know exactly what they want their draft to say. Instead, they will start writing and let the writing lead them toward what they need to know for the first draft. Notice: they may postpone the *drafting*, but they do not postpone the *writing* and *planning*.

Notice that legal writing, like other writing, has voice and communicates attitudes toward the reader.

Writing conveys voice and an attitude toward the reader—often summed up as "tone." The tone of legal writing can be crucial to its effectiveness or lack thereof. Tone is created in many ways, some of them subtle. At various points in this book, we will point out how tone affects effectiveness. In the last chapter, we will show how diction affects tone. Here we simply recommend that lawyers begin to pay attention to how tone is created in the writing they read and how this contributes to or detracts from effectiveness.

As we said above, effective legal writers do not ordinarily write in ways that call attention to themselves or their abilities. This does not mean, however, that effective legal writing

The poet William Stafford was asked if he was ever troubled by writer's block. "Oh, no," he said. "I just lower my standards."

is necessarily *impersonal* writing. In a particular situation, an impersonal tone may be what is most effective. Lawyers asking the judge to sanction an opponent, for example, do not want to appear to be personally offended by the malefactions they are alleging. In other situations, however, in letters to bereaved clients, for example, an impersonal tone could work against effectiveness. A professional tone is not necessarily an impersonal one.

In every case, effective legal writing will be passionately committed writing. The key is what it is passionate *about*. In writing to a judge or jury during a trial, the effective lawyer will convey a personal commitment to the task of helping the decision-maker reach the right decision. Effective legal writing demonstrates a passionate commitment to professional performance.

Understand That Revision Is Crucial to Effective Writing

Some people seem to think that good writers revise less than the rest of us. It's the other way around. Good writers revise more. Effective writers know that it is not when they draft but when they revise that they are able to do the most to make their writing count for a reader.

In this discussion, *revision* means more than editing or "polishing." It means something more like "rethinking." It is an action that takes place before, not just after drafting. When it takes place afterwards, it doesn't just tinker with drafts: it doesn't hesitate to dump them and start over, or turn them back to front, or cut big chunks and start writing again from the good bits. It aims not just to "polish" but to transform writing.

Effective revision includes proofreading for correctness and accuracy. Poor proofreading seriously reduces effectiveness. Many lawyers could become more effective simply by proofreading more carefully. But effective legal writers will revise with more than correctness in mind.

Most lawyers know that revision is important. The excuse some lawyers offer for not doing it is that they don't have time.

Lawyers do write under pressure, often a lot of pressure, and they need to find ways of writing efficiently, as well as

A paralegal told us that in a firm she worked for, her boss had to defend herself because she often asked our informant to rewrite documents. "Her partner thought her use of me as an 'editor' or 'writer' was a waste of valuable paralegal time and increased paper costs." We suspect that partner will not be among those who buy this book.

effectively. Revision can seem to be inefficient. It will seem so particularly to writers who don't see it making much difference. The advice in this book will help you see how to revise so as to make a real difference.

If a writer has procrastinated long enough, revision isn't inefficient, it's impossible. We suspect that some unconfident writers procrastinate in order to make it impossible to revise. They will need to learn that efficiency *and* effectiveness—of thinking and of writing—are increased when we learn to write early instead of waiting until we feel ready to produce a final draft.

All the good lawyers and effective legal writers we know make time to revise. It's do-able, even in the pressure cooker of the law office. If you want to be effective as a legal writer, you will do it as much as you can.

Use the Available Technologies—and Recognize their Limitations

In this section,
> Dictating Machines
> Word Processors
> Fax Machines and Email
> Document Assembly and Expert Systems

Pencils, pens, markers, different colors of ink, erasers, scissors, different kinds of paper, tape, storyboards—all are technologies for writers, although in this electronic age we may not think of them as such.

Almost every lawyer today employs some of the electronic technologies: photocopiers, dictation machines, word processors, fax machines, email, electronic databases. Some use document assembly software and expert systems. Each of these technologies can help lawyers write more effectively. All can also promote ineffective writing—even the photocopier, with its capacity to reproduce our mistakes *ad nauseum*. Some cautions are in order.

Dictating machines. Revise a paper copy of everything you dictate at least once before sending it out. Dictating machines, and the workers who transcribe their contents,

---

Judge Chambers thought that opinions would improve if judges had to write them on a chunk of granite with a hammer and chisel. I guess I don't have to say that he thought most opinions were too long.

allow us to get our talk down on paper. This makes these machines useful for gathering thoughts, for producing rough summaries of conferences for one's own use, and for getting the roughest of rough drafts started. But dictated texts, like talk, are almost always puffy and unfocused. They are organized more like a conversation with oneself than like a well-thought-out argument or request for action. Lawyers should not expect to be able to dictate even the simplest letter in final form, let alone a contract, or motion. Everything that is dictated should be reviewed in hard copy in the expectation that significant changes will be made. Transcribers should be told not to put dictation into "final" form. In our experience, secretaries did not mind making many drafts of a document, even before the days before word processing, as long as they weren't being told that each one was the "final" draft. They could use cheaper paper for the earlier versions too.

Remember, though, that reading a *written* document into a dictation machine is a form of reading aloud: it can help us hear the places where the text might be improved.

Word Processors. *Always revise a* printed *version of any document composed on a word processor before calling it finished.*

Word processors allow us to revise more easily. We can cut, paste, delete, re-order, add, and the document will be reformatted automatically. These virtues give rise to two dangers, however. One is that if we review our documents only on a screen, we will miss mistakes and other infelicities that appear when we review them on paper. The other is that our nicely reformatted print-outs will look a lot more finished than they are.

Proofread in hard copy any documents produced on the word processor. Do not just "spell-check" them or proofread them on screen. Printouts of *word-processed documents usually contain more errors than do documents that were typed.* Spell-checkers miss many spelling and typographical errors, as we show in Chapter Six: Rewrite for Effectiveness. Also,

Not long ago, law offices had stenographers for dictation, and electric typewriters and carbon paper were essential. You'd have to go to a museum to see those now. There are still some lawyers and secretaries who can remember the day when if you made a change in the original, you had to change all the carbons. One of the C's in the FCC code in emails refers to "carbons." I wonder what some young people make of that.

when we make changes on the word processor, the automatic reformatting often produces infelicities we notice only in printouts.

Integrate—do not simply import—language from other files and databases. Word processors allow us easily to import other writing into our documents—our own, our associates', forms from formbooks, language from statutes and cases. Many legal documents are now bloated with such language, language that has not been culled and integrated effectively. Such "easy" writing makes damned hard reading, to paraphrase Mark Twain. We offer advice on how to integrate citations in "Rewrite for Effective Quotation and Citation" in Chapter Six (pp. 162-168).

Review for over-all structure and organization using paper copies. It is hard to check for structure and organization on the word processor for the simple reason that you can't flip pages easily. The good news is that once we see from reading the printed version how we need to change the structure and organization, we can easily make the changes using the word processor.

Fax Machines and Email. *Don't respond to fax and email messages for 24 hours,* especially if they have made you angry, even a little bit. Fax machines and email allow a quick response, which is precisely why they can contribute to ineffective writing. We discuss this further in the section on letters in Chapter Two, "Writing through the Day" (pp. 35-44).

> I can always tell when a design has been produced on the computer. The designer ends up working with the elements offered by the software instead of with a concept.
>
> —Head of a graphic design firm

Electronic Databases. *Don't let the database limit your ideas.* Be sure you are working from your own concept of your case, not from the elements provided by the database. As we become more sophisticated about word processing software, search engines, and other electronic resources, we are realizing that each offers only its particular way of coming to terms with a problem, not the only way. This is true of all technologies, of course. If you are a hammer, everything looks like a nail. The more effective lawyers will keep their tools from limiting their vision.

Document Assembly and Expert Systems. Computer software is available now that enables lawyers to "automate" the process of creating documents they produce frequently—from certain standard letters, to powers of attorney, to more complex documents like leases, wills, and trust documents. At the simplest level, lawyers can design macros in a word processing program to format letters and other documents. At a more complex level are the "expert systems," which are large expensive packages that provide templates for documents in a particular area of practice—like Estate Planning—along with questions that develop options and guide choices for the person assembling the document. Some of these systems provide hyperlinks to pertinent statutes and commentary. In the middle of this range are software packages that allow lawyers to construct their own templates out of documents they themselves have written.

When templates have been created, lawyers can "assemble" documents very quickly by responding to the questions the program asks about the "variables"—such as the names of the testator, testator's children, their birth dates, and so forth. When the variables are entered, the click of a button can produce a whole document, properly formatted and complete with Table of Contents.

"Assembling" documents in this way is not *writing* them, in the way the term is used in this book. In document assembly, the *writing* takes place when the lawyer creates and revises the document on which the template will be based, and when the lawyer organizes the decision structure for the template. It happens also when the lawyer revises a document that has been assembled or revises the template.

The main promise of document assembly systems is greatly increased efficiency. Once they are in place, they can cut drastically the time necessary to produce certain documents. They can allow legal assistants who are "document producers" to generate drafts that can then be revised by senior lawyers. They can also help lawyers and law firms produce documents that are more consistent with each other and that have a more professional appearance. A pro-

It took me, I'd say, a hundred hours to design the template for the A/B trust I just produced for you in five minutes.

—A lawyer demonstrating document assembly

fessional appearance is important to client satisfaction, and thus to effective legal writing.

Before the document assembly software can do any of this, however, the templates must be designed and debugged, which is the time-consuming and expensive part of the process.

Since here we are concerned primarily with what makes legal writing effective, we will leave aside questions of how much time these programs can eventually save. This would no doubt vary with the lawyer and the practice.

Are documents assembled by these programs more effective? The answer obviously depends on

- whether the document from which the template was constructed was effectively written in the first place,

- whether the template is up-to-date, and

- whether the template addresses the situation of *this* client appropriately.

Inexperienced lawyers will be forced to rely on the experts behind the expert systems and may not know as much about these experts as they would like, just as they don't know much about who made the forms in the form books. Experienced lawyers who have written documents they have found effective will probably want to design their own templates and be the ones responsible for keeping them up to date—provided they are comfortable doing the necessary programming.

In any case, legal writers must remember that documents assembled in these ways will still need to be revised:

Accuracy in the information that has been entered will need to be checked. The good news is that if it is accurate in one place, it will be accurate in all the other places where it occurs.

Some provisions automatically supplied by the program may need to be cut. This is easily enough done, of course, if you know what to cut, and properly reformatted versions of the documents can be very quickly reproduced.

If the templates have been well-designed and reworked sufficiently, the documents they produce will be 90% right 90% of the time. That's the standard I strive for.

—A lawyer adept at document assembly programs

I find that I am constantly making small revisions in templates. Mostly, they are in one of two categories: 1. A small correction to the logic (I might have thought of a better way to formulate a gender-correction, for example), or 2. A language correction (as when the law changes, or I attend a seminar where they suggest a change, for example).

—A lawyer adept in document assembly programs

Provisions pertinent to this client's needs may need to be added addressing items (like specific bequests outside the family) that were complex enough or rare enough that you or the experts decided not to provide cues for them in the template.

Templates themselves need to be revised from time to time. Lawyers relying on expert systems pay to have the experts do this. Unhappily, when you use expert systems, you may not be able to preserve particular changes you have made in templates. Lawyers who design their own templates from their own documents can change them as they think necessary.

Lawyers must consider the costs and benefits of implementing document assembly systems beyond those that format standard letters. Evidence is growing, however, that the investment can pay off, especially for the larger firms.

Writing and Effective Billing

Today lawyers must pay more attention to how they write their bills than in the past.

Effective billing is billing that leaves the client satisfied with the value received. The billing that does this will vary with the lawyer, the client, and the legal situation. When the value received by the client is obvious to the client and the amount of the bill obviously appropriate, the line item can still read "For legal services rendered." Lawyers can help make the value of the services apparent by, among other things, staying in touch with the client, and by sending them copies of all papers prepared. In a good many situations, however, clients will want more detail than this. The question is always how much detail and what kind.

Generally the more detail in bills the better. Some clients, like insurance companies, have begun to get quite specific about the kind of detail they want. They provide categories and codes and may employ external audit firms to scrutinize bills. They may require that attorneys get prior approval for some activities, including "research." One set of guidelines from an insurance company lists among its "unacceptable" fees "Excessive revision and editing" (They

Consider the bill the climax of the lawyer-client relationship—its power to build or destroy that relationship should not be underestimated.

—J. Harris Morgan, *How to Draft Bills that Clients Rush to Pay*, ABA, 1995

At the old firm, I once went through decades of old railroad files before they were sent out for destruction. Before the 1970s, the common practice was to send out a single bill at the end of the case with a single entry, "For legal services rendered ..." and the dollar amount. Sometimes the name of the case or the dates of service would be added. That invoice with a short cover letter would be the second-to-last paper in the file. The last would be a transmittal from the client paying the bill.

—A senior partner

Clients may not mind being billed $5000 for "Working on brief," particularly if they were sent a copy of the brief.

—A lawyer

You do have to screen clients. Some will complain about everything.

—A trial lawyer

17

If you have a good product and a good turn-around time, you'll be all right.

—A lawyer in general practice

The current generation of lawyers can hardly imagine practicing law without billing by the hour. Yet many other modes have been around longer than hourly billing and are still in use—fixed fees, retainers, and contingent fees. These and other options, properly designed, remove the skewed incentives of hourly billing, and replace them with incentives to handle matters in ways that meet the requirement of Federal Rule 1 for a "just speedy, and inexpensive determination of every action."

—John W. Toothman, "Real Reform," ABA, Sept 1995, 80

Well-drafted bills are laced with action verbs like: *filed, mailed, copied, authored, deposed, contacted, secured, determined, concluded, improved, rejected, proposed, suggested, calculated, examined, compared, searched, researched, briefed, drafted, prepared, constructed, closed, engaged, demanded, compiled, revised, updated redacted.*

—A lawyer who does CLE on billing

18

don't say when the revision and editing becomes "excessive") and "Proofreading for spelling errors," which is considered a "clerical activity." Lawyers employed by such clients must abide by the billing schemes they require.

Lawyers who are not working under these restrictions should think about how best to communicate value in billing. Increasingly, it is being recognized that *a notation of the time expended by the lawyer is an inadequate measure of the value of the lawyer's work.* More effective lawyers do more in less time. Lawyers can spend time working for clients that they can't bill—trying unsuccessfully to make phone calls, for example. The brief time expended preparing a document using a well-designed document assembly system obviously fails to capture value.

When it comes to value, clients as a rule are less concerned with the amount of time expended than with

- the lawyer's concern for and attention to the client's case,

- the lawyer's professionalism—honesty, ethics, and competence, and

- the lawyer's effort.

These values are communicated by more than the bill. They are communicated, for example, by keeping the client apprised—often by letter—of progress or delay and by sending the client copies of papers prepared in the case. But the bill itself can help. Helpful bills do the following:

- Provide a narrative of all of the actions undertaken in the client's behalf (including unsuccessful attempts to make phone calls, for example). To be in a position to do this, lawyers must learn to keep good time sheets *making entries at the time they perform the actions.* The general rule is the more detail the better on such sheets, though there is a point of diminishing returns.

- Structure the narrative of these actions in a way that reflects the continuous attention given to the client's case, that is, not in piecemeal column entries by date, but in a continuous listing of action items.

Effective Writing

- Use the language of action.

- Use descriptive terms judiciously to give the reader a proper appreciation of the effort involved in and the value of the action.

What are effective terms for the kinds of efforts made by effective writers? Communicating the effort involved in effective writing may not be as straightforward a matter as it might seem. The picture is complicated further by the advent of billing codes and of firms that do outside audits of bills for big clients.

In describing the actions that produce effective legal writing

- It is probably not a good idea to bill for "briefing" cases. This term of art from law school refers to actions better described in action terms for non-lawyers as *research, collect, summarize, digest*, and *analyze*.

- To provide more detail than that offered in "worked on brief," you can use terms like *planned, drafted, constructed, improved, revised, edited, checked for accuracy*. Some lawyers appear to think that "proofreading" for correctness should be done by clerical staff. We think it should be done by the lawyers signing the document. You can use the term *editing* to include the proofreading you quite appropriately do.

- The word *prepare* may be reserved for writing activities that are essentially clerical. Lawyers *draft* documents; secretaries *prepare* them.

Writing is not something that should always be billed by the clock. Some of the more formal tasks, like brief-writing, can be billed that way. If you are asked by a corporate client to digest cases according to a format that requires extra time, you are advised always to follow the guidelines you are given, spend the extra time, and bill accordingly. You might consider attaching a letter that explains why so much time was necessary.

In cases that don't involve a lot of money, let's say a $5,000 accident case, you may be required to spend more time on writing than it would be ethical to bill for. Once

Seldom refer to a telephone call as only that. It deserves the dignity of a "conference" in billing. But don't say "Conference with defendant's lawyer," or worse, "Conference." Say "Telephone conference with defendant's lawyer to discuss temporary child support award and to determine the date on which the defendant will begin to make payments."

—A lawyer who does CLE on billing

What lawyers do is read, write, listen, talk. That's all we do. That's not what we would say on the bill though.

—A trial lawyer

You wouldn't want to bill for "Going to library to check on a cite," even though that kind of accuracy is absolutely essential.

—A trial lawyer

I use four categories: *Begin draft, Prepare, Edit,* and *Finalize,* which is checking the exhibits and so forth. I don't use the word *writing*. My partner uses *Read and Analyze, Prepare Response, Revise/Edit.* We have another partner who goes into much more detail.

—An experienced trial lawyer

19

> When I'm writing a brief, I can just let the clock run.
>
> —A trial lawyer

> I've had complaints about bills for conferences that involved a lot of lawyers. I've never had a complaint about writing.
>
> —A trial lawyer

> The client and I just couldn't get together. His idea of a retainer was a lien on his Mercedes—if the previous attorney would release his lien
>
> —A trial lawyer

you take a case, you are ethically obligated to spend the time needed for effective writing and representation, even though you can't properly bill for it. Your bill can reflect the effort and time expended, of course, and may generate good will.

We claim above that effective writers always get help from others with their writing. This kind of consultation may not be billable as such if you have auditors who require unitary billing or who tend to be critical of multi-lawyer "conferences."

It is common practice in firms with a number of lawyers to let an associate do a draft which a senior lawyer then revises and edits, bringing to bear his or her experience about what will make it persuasive for a judge, maybe even for a particular judge. There is usually no problem with billing for this writing at the two different rates.

Clients are always unhappy to get bills in amounts greater than they expected. The amount of the bill, it seems, is less important than what the amount was *expected* to be. At the beginning of a matter, lawyers should always give clients an idea of what the bill will be, and they should let clients know immediately when it appears that an initial estimate will be exceeded.

② Writing through the Day

Lawyers write. They write all day long, all kinds of things. Some writing tasks they are just beginning to think about or research, some they are putting into final form. Often they are revising and editing writing—their own or that of an associate or paralegal. They dictate, bang away on the word processor, write in longhand on legal pads. They are always scratching out notes, and, of course, filling out time sheets.

Some of this writing requires a lot of thought, some of it can be pretty formulaic. Some has to be finished up right now, or sooner, to meet deadlines set by statute or otherwise. Some will be done in short bursts and revisited later. Some requires sustained writing for periods of time. This sustained writing may have to be done very early in the day or on the weekend since during the day lawyers are often interrupted by telephone calls or visits from clients and colleagues, episodes which themselves are likely to generate writing.

A lawyer's life is a writing life, but rarely do lawyers write in what we might have thought was the ideal writing situation. Effective legal writing does not happen by accident. If it happens, it happens because a lawyer has found a way—in the midst of many other demands—to give his or her writing the attention required. Effective writing is a significant achievement—one that, in our view, might even deserve to be called a heroic achievement. Lawyers who have been practicing for a while know this: that's why a reputation as an effective legal writer carries so much weight in the profession.

In the first and last chapters of this book we show how lawyers can manage the writing process to make effective legal writing possible in their often hectic working circumstances. In this chapter we take a look at some crucial domains of effective legal writing that get short shrift in law school even though all lawyers deal with them every day: facts, forms, and letters.

Facts

In this section,
> The Practice of Fact
> How to Develop Facts
> How to Give Telling Accounts of Facts
>> Let the Facts Speak for Themselves
>> Do Not Offer the Opponent's Version
>> When You Have "Bad" Facts, Do Not Pretend
>> They Aren't There

The Practice of Fact

In law school, the facts are a given, and the student's task is to apply and argue the law, not to develop or argue the facts. In the practice of law, things are very different. In the law office, the new law clerk assigned a legal problem finds that the facts are at best sketchily stated. The new lawyer encounters a professional world where the facts are often meager, or uncertain, or forgotten.

Lawyers quickly learn that in trials or negotiations what is wanted is good facts, first of all, and when you have them, it will be the facts you argue most strongly.

New lawyers do know to begin by developing the facts of the case. But this is rarely as straightforward a business as they might have thought. Facts continue to emerge as a matter progresses. Nearly every experienced lawyer has been embarrassed by a decisive fact coming to light on the eve of trial, or during it.

The good news is that while lawyers can know, or learn, just about all the law that applies to a particular sort of situation, no two cases are exactly alike in their facts. In litigation, business planning, or negotiations, the need to become educated on the facts of the individual case is what keeps the practice interesting.

Here we focus on how to develop the facts with a client and how to use writing to help with this task. We also give guidelines for how to present the facts effectively in argument. Developing facts in written discovery is dealt with in the chapter on Writing through the Trial.

How to Develop Facts

As soon as a new matter comes to you, start a skeleton chronology of the facts as they appear at this stage. Leave a broad margin or make a separate column in which you can note the witnesses or instruments that will prove particular facts.

Clients know the facts that brought them into the office, but they tend to be caught up in emotion and probably don't realize what facts are important to the legal resolution of the case. In the beginning, the lawyer doesn't either. Sometimes clients will be intent upon facts that clearly are irrelevant legally—the fact that their domestic partner is ungrateful, perhaps. Clients will not be happy if you dismiss such matters as unimportant. Remember that you must respect what the client wants to accomplish.

Lawyers, like everyone else, can fail to develop the facts adequately because they jump too early to a theory of the case. Lawyers should listen to their clients and hear them out, even if the facts the client is reciting appear to be irrelevant and immaterial. Clients, like the rest of us, like to be listened to.

If you recap the facts to your client now and again as you listen, you show you are listening, and you also create the opportunity to be corrected where you have heard wrong.

Let the client start the tale where he or she wants. Don't interrupt except to invite more facts. When the client has completed the chronology, you can go back and ask for facts that fill in gaps or develop particular areas. As new facts emerge, you can add them to this chronology and strike out the ones that appear to be irrelevant. In some cases—often in estate planning, for example—lawyers may ask clients

> We had exactly the same facts in this case, except for who the clients were. One client loved the fight, and the other just wanted to get the business behind him. The first one got more money, the other one got out of it earlier. It's not clear that one "did better" than the other one.
>
> —A trial lawyer

to write out some facts in response to questions the lawyer provides.

When it comes time to write a legal memorandum or a negotiation letter, make another list of the facts that places them in order of importance.

In a case where the facts have become quite complicated, lawyers will need to find other ways of organizing facts. It may then be useful to develop headings to organize them. The headings finally will be provided by the particular issues you decide to argue but it may take a while to discover these.

Writers of long nonfiction works face a similar problem of organization. The highly respected writer of nonfiction, John McPhee, organizes his facts using a method that might be adapted by lawyers even though their purposes are different. McPhee makes handwritten notes in the field and the library, types up these notes and makes a photocopy of them, then cuts up the photocopied material and files notes in folders according to his intuitive sense of what materials belong together. At first he may not know why they belong together; he just feels that they do. Later a conscious rationale will emerge. He labels each file, sometimes with a nonsense word. Once the material is in these files, McPhee is able to see more readily what gaps need to be filed by further research and work in the field. He can also begin to consider what would be the best order for presenting the material. Lawyers in complex cases may find useful some variation on this method.

How to Give Telling Accounts of Facts

An effectively written account of the facts may be the most telling resource a lawyer has in making an argument to a judge or another lawyer. How should you proceed when it comes time to produce these accounts?

There is no form for facts. *Facts should be presented as a story. Whenever you give an account of the facts, tell the story as simply as you can, using only material facts, and acknowledging facts in dispute.*

The experienced lawyer who found the new lawyer looking for a form for the facts advised him to write out the facts

I once noticed a new lawyer looking through a form file. "What are you looking for?" I asked. "A form for the facts," the new lawyer replied.

—A senior partner

24

in a letter to his mother. This is not a bad way of getting in the right frame of mind for giving an account of the facts of a case. In a letter to your mother, you are not likely to violate the principle that *a statement of the facts should not look as if a lawyer wrote it.* Telling your mother or another lay person about a case can help you clear out the legalistic overtones. This kind of exercise can also help a lawyer focus upon the *material* facts. It can restore to a lawyer buried in the details of the case a sense of the fundamental facts a person unfamiliar with a case needs to get a grasp upon it.

Lawyers are usually good storytellers, though they sometimes don't bring their skills to bear on their presentations of facts in writing. *Stories* are about *people*, not about "plaintiffs," "appellants," "claimants," and so forth. Well-told stories use concrete details and vivid images. They *show* rather than *tell*. They make chronologies clear, but they do not just string facts together in chronological order. They *give a narrative a sense of direction and purpose.*

In telling the story of the facts of the case, a lawyer's purpose is not to entertain the reader or listener, nor is it to tell "the whole story," even if such a thing were possible. It is to set out the undisputed facts material to the question that must be decided. A lawyer's recital of facts may be inclined ever-so-slightly in favor of the lawyer's client without doing any harm. But *don't fudge the facts.* In a case arising out of a car crash, don't say that your client was stopped at the stop sign if there is testimony that your client was backing up when the accident happened.

By the time briefs are being written at trial, the facts are in (except for the surprises we mentioned above). In presenting facts to judges, *lawyers must be aware of what are the **material** facts, as opposed to those that are merely **relevant**, and stick to the material facts.* This is harder than it sounds. You can decide what is material only when you have a clear sense of how you are going to argue your case. It may take a while to get clear about this, and your sense may change during the case. Ideally you will have a strong theory of the case at the beginning of the argument and will not change it at trial. It is not always possible to realize this ideal.

What is material may be different when matters are presented to a jury rather than to a judge. A very successful personal injury lawyer from Los Angeles who was suing my client, a billion-dollar railroad, once told me, "The difference between us is that you are a law lawyer, and I am a fact-and-person lawyer. My client violated a safety regulation. Contributory negligence bars him from recovery. But the fact is he lost his arm at the shoulder and is permanently disabled and suffers phantom pain in the hand he lost—and that's why you will be paying me a lot of money, regardless of laws, regulations, and rules."

He produced an attractive young Hungarian neurologist who testified that in her opinion the plaintiff did indeed suffer pain in the lost hand, that it was real pain, and that the condition, called "causalgia," had first been studied in the Civil War when soldiers lost important parts of their bodies from cannon balls.

He did indeed collect a lot of money.

—A trial lawyer

Here's an argument to a jury made in a story that handles a bad fact well:

"George had been to a party, and he had had a pretty good time. He was, to put it plainly, drunk when he left the party. And he was drunk when he crossed the street. But George was one of those persons who knew when he was drunk. You have seen them— supercautious, superslow people. Well, we can all tell such people are drunk because they are overly cautious and overly careful.

And so George came to the crossing and the green light was with him. There is no question about that. More than half a dozen witnesses saw him crossing with the light. And, when he was helplessly trapped in the center of the street, Mr. Majors here, the defendant, came careening and screeching around the corner at a high rate of speed, nearly tipped his car over, ran the red light, and ran poor George down like a mangy cur.

Now, George was drunk all right. But the laws of this country were passed to protect both the drunk and the sober. One does not lose one's rights as a citizen because one crosses the street with the green light while drunk. As a matter of fact, if you think about it, a drunk man like George needed the protection of the law more than a sober man would under the same circumstances."

The lawyer who told this story comments: "I would not have achieved the favorable result in the case for George had I held George's drunkenness back, tried to cover it, and objected like hell to the introduction as evidence of George's blood alcohol level of .18 taken in the emergency room a half-hour after the accident."

—Gerry Spence, *How to Argue and Win Every Time*, New York: St. Martins P, 1995, 132.

Let the facts speak for themselves, even with juries. Don't use nouns that prejudge the matter—"violated the law in a despicable manner" as opposed to "hit 4-year-old Joe Valdez while driving 60 miles an hour in a school zone"—or gild your words with adjectives that you hope will give them emphasis—"*egregious* violation," "*brutal* behavior," "*reckless* disregard," "*obvious* omission." Facts speak most powerfully when they speak for themselves and readers can draw for themselves the desired inference about the quality of the deed. *Never fudge the facts*. It's fatal.

When you are speaking or writing to a judge, do not begin by reciting the facts. In every legal argument, *first explain the nature of the case and what the court is being asked to decide.* At the beginnings of judicial opinions, we often find a long narrative of the factual "background" of the case. This is not a good model for lawyers. Lawyers who read these accounts know that they often find themselves asking, "Background to what? What is being decided here?" This is just what lawyers should tell judges before reciting any more than the

few facts that may be necessary to understand the issue that is being decided.

Do not offer the opponent's version. You may do a better job than they do. After setting out what the court is being asked to decide, state, as concisely as possible, the material facts supporting your case.

When you have "bad" facts, do not pretend they aren't there. This gives your opponent the opportunity to make it seem that you are fudging the facts. You can de-emphasize bad facts by mentioning them in unemphatic places—the middles of paragraphs, for example. You can also de-emphasize them by stating them as claims or testimony rather than fact: "Jones testified that my client's fingerprints were on the knife," rather than, "My client's fingerprints were on the murder weapon."

Argue the facts on every possible occasion—if they favor your client.

> It was a multi-party anti-trust trial. The lawyers filling the courtroom were warming up to argue several motions when the judge called over a lawyer he knew. The lawyer had sat in the jury box because there was no room at the counsels' tables.
>
> "Okay, Mike," he said. "What's going on here?"
>
> What lawyer would not be glad to have that reputation with a judge—a reputation for being able to set out "what's going on here" in a succinct, clear and trustworthy way?

Facts Checklist

- Develop facts for yourself first chronologically and then revise them in order of importance as you develop your theory of the case.

- Distinguish *material* from merely *relevant* facts, and in arguing to judges, stick to the material facts.

- Before narrating facts to judges, let them know what the court is being asked to decide.

- Present the facts as a simple story, not as something that looks like a lawyer wrote it.

- Let the facts speak for themselves.

- Do not state your opponent's version.

- Never fudge the facts.

- Do not fail to mention "bad" facts, but mention them in unemphatic ways.

- Argue the facts on every possible occasion—if they favor your client.

Forms

In this section,

The Temptations of Forms

Forms [May Not] Cover the Bases

Forms [May Not] Save Time

Consider the Sources of Forms

Forms from Formbooks and Commercial Data
Banks

Printed Forms

Forms Custom-Made by You

Forms From Your Office's Data Bank

When Not to Use a Form

How to Revise Forms Effectively

> "Sir, the law is as I
> say it is ... and we
> have several set forms
> which are held as
> law, and so held and
> used for good reason,
> though we cannot at
> present remember that
> reason."
>
> —Sir John Fortescue,
> C.J. 1394, 1476, *de
> laudibus legum*

> I challenged him to
> tell me the difference
> between a "will" and a
> "testament."
> "Well," he said. "I
> don't know that there
> is one. But I'm sure
> not going to change
> the formula. If I do,
> something is sure to
> go wrong."
>
> —A lawyer

> Writing isn't magic.
> But then magic isn't
> magic either.
>
> —A Pulitzer Prize-
> winning author

Forms represent an attempt to impose uniformity on situations. They are an inescapable feature of any institution or bureaucracy, including, of course, a law office. Lawyers are sometimes compelled to use particular forms by statute, court rule, or by the reporting requirements of a client insurance company, for example. But lawyers resort to forms on many occasions when they don't have to. It is important to recognize how forms can help and hinder effective writing.

A form, by definition, was developed on some other occasion for some other situation. That in itself should be enough to create caution about their use. But forms can come to partake of the aura of the doctrine of *stare decisis*—the notion that what was held to govern a situation in the past should govern a similar situation now. Lawyers in common law systems are trained to honor this doctrine, which may help explain why some forms with obvious deficiencies have the tenacity they do.

Forms may get some of their attractiveness from the human tendency to engage in magical thinking. Magical thinking assumes that it is the formulas themselves that are effective, not anything they actually say. Abracadabra, you're a corporation.

Some members of the public seem to think that lawyers are sorcerers who trade in magical formulas and suspect that lawyers complicate matters that could be handled by anyone who knew the formula. This is the suspicion that creates the market for how-to-do-it kits that offer ways to get by without lawyers. Packages like these have been with us for a long time. Benjamin Franklin's print shop in Philadelphia sold printed legal forms as early as 1775.

Lawyers know that treating forms as if they were magic can produce unhappy results down the line, like those encountered by the sorcerer's apprentice. But lawyers too can attribute magical power to forms, especially when they are working in an area not familiar to them.

> Indeed, a good kit might be better than a bad lawyer.
>
> —A judge

The Temptations of Forms

Forms [May Not] Cover the Bases. Lawyers commonly resort to forms in the hope that this will keep them from leaving out anything important. Some will. Many will not.

A formbook published in 1991 offers the following language for an agreement to purchase services:

> Whereas first party is desirous of obtaining the services offered by second party and to sell second party certain accounts receivable, notes, drafts, acceptances, leases, mortgages, contracts and choses in action. . . .

The form fails to mention deeds of trust, which are used more often than mortgages in many states.

The formidable release form quoted below includes twenty-three types of claim—including an "extent," which is a debt due the Queen. It omits fraud, negligence, or other tort, and hence excludes them from the release:

> In consideration of payment by X to you of Y, you agree to release and forever discharge X, its predecessor and successor partnerships, and all present and former partners, principals, employees and agents, and their respective heirs, executors, administrators, successors and assigns (collectively, the "releasees"), jointly and severally, of and from all manner of actions, causes of actions, suits, debts, dues, sums of money, accounts, reckonings, bonds, bills, specialties, contracts, controversies, agreements,

covenants, promises, variances, trespasses, damages, judgments, extents, executions, claims and demands whatsoever, in law, in admiralty or in equity. . . .

Published forms usually do list a great many specific items. The lawyers relying on them had better hope that these long lists are exhaustive. If they aren't, they are more likely to come under the principle *expressio unius est exclusio alterius* (The mention of one thing implies exclusion of the other).

Forms [May Not] Save Time. Lawyers use forms for agreements from data banks, thinking that this will save time. But forms almost always add unnecessary matter and make the document more complicated and less clear than necessary. Time may be wasted when all is said and done because of the time spent reviewing and negotiating.

> One of the forms we use for a Power of Attorney was prepared by Peterson, Brooks, Steiner & Wisk. I know that's an old one because they sponsored a semi-pro baseball team I played for in the '30's. It covers "bottomry," which, by the way, is the power to charter sailboats.
>
> —A senior partner

> My office was handling a tax-free exchange of real estate under a provision of the Internal Revenue Code. It required our client to convey his property to a sort of escrow agent and the other party to do the same. The agent would then complete the conveyance. It wasn't complicated. A partner in my office set this up in a contract of two and one-half pages. The other party, one of the large banks, represented by a large firm, and apparently by a young lawyer in that firm, presented a seventy-three-page contract, with enough computer-generated boilerplate in fine print to torpedo-proof an aircraft carrier. The contract was not for us to approve: it was sent to us merely for information. It was a pathetic demonstration of the tendency to assume that if the computer generated it, it must be okay. Even more pathetic: my partner will probably present a statement for two hours and the bank's lawyer will charge it for twenty hours.
>
> —A senior partner

Consider the Sources of Forms

Lawyers use forms from several sources.

- Forms from formbooks and commercial data banks

- Printed forms

- Forms from your office's memory bank

- Forms custom-made by you

Each raises special considerations when it comes to effective legal writing.

Forms from Formbooks and Commercial Data Banks. Too much cannot be said about the deficiencies of forms in formbooks and commercial data banks. Formbooks are written by paralegals or non-practicing lawyers employed by the law book companies. The forms are extracted from appellate decisions in which legal documents or statutes are being construed. The documents are being construed in appellate decisions because they are ambiguous, vague, equivocal, or unintelligible. A document that has to be interpreted on one point may be problematic on other points not addressed by the court. But the whole document is taken up by the formbook publishers.

Forms provided in expert systems may be vouched for by experts. Updates will be a part of the package you pay for. But in the nature of things these forms will tend to err on the side of unnecessary complexity. Lawyers are usually more afraid of leaving something out than of putting too much in.

Printed Forms. Printed forms can be effective legal writing—when they include the necessary provisions—because they can expedite a transaction. They tend not to be as thoroughly scrutinized. Finally, they cannot be imperceptibly altered.

Lay people often do not realize that every printed form is slanted, consciously or unconsciously, in favor of one party or the other, depending on who paid for the printing.

Forms from Your Office's Data Bank. Existing forms can be used as a checklist for content. But they should not be used blindly, even if they have been created by a respected partner or expert on the subject. The law changes rapidly today, and the forms in your office's memory bank may be obsolete. Even if you have handled a similar case for a similar client, and created a form that is embedded in the memory bank, you should approach every problem as if it were brand new.

> I don't claim any credit for it, but only once have I been asked to supply material to a formbook company. That was in a case in which one of my partners had made a serious mistake in a matter, and I was elected to try to bail him out. I finally got to the court of appeals, which did rule in his favor, although for the wrong reason. A formbook company wrote asking for the pleadings and documents, provided I would not spend more than $20 in xeroxing, and in return offered to give me credit and the volume in which the forms were published. I could buy the other ninety-nine volumes if I wished.
> —A senior partner

> After a time, experienced practitioners realize that many clients have more confidence in printers than they do in lawyers.
> —A senior partner

A partner in a large law firm was approaching retirement and was not, unfortunately, on good terms with the firm. He was presented with a lengthy retirement contract, which he executed and returned.

Some months later an issue arose concerning the retiring partner's duties. The partner who had drafted the contract noticed for the first time that it had been altered by clauses added at the ends of paragraphs in the same font, in ways that did not make him happy, needless to say.

—A senior partner

In a jurisdiction noted for the integrity of its judges and the wisdom of its lawyers, a certain printed form for a quitclaim deed has been standard for over fifty years. Unfortunately, the form uses the word *convey*, which in that jurisdiction implies certain warranties, and converts the deed from a quitclaim to a limited warranty deed.

—A real estate lawyer

The printed real estate contract—usually entitled "Preliminary Sales Agreement" or "Deposit Receipt"—is prepared by the real estate broker's association. It is designed to make sure the commission is paid even if the deal falls through. It is not challenged by the parties usually because (a) the seller has been promised more for his property than he ever dreamed, and (b) the buyer, by paying a tiny amount of earnest money, has the land tied up until he or she can peddle it to someone else, or (c) the seller is willing to give it away to get off the mortgage.

—A real estate lawyer

Forms Custom-Made by You. No two clients are exactly alike, and no two fact situations are identical, so ideally every office transaction will be individually tailored. The greater ease of access to forms may make the lawyers who craft their own instruments even more of an endangered species than they are now. Creating your own instruments requires skill, experience, and self-confidence.

Electronic technology has given lawyers unprecedented access to forms. Lawyers can now quickly search large data bases inside and outside their offices and generate any number of forms, and these can easily be imported into documents the lawyer is working on, without even having to reread to see if the material was copied correctly. Many lawyers and judges are convinced that this will make the writing of lawyers even more bloated and unintelligible than it has been.

The easy access to many *different* forms, however, may keep lawyers from having to rely too readily on any one form they might find, and may help awaken their sense of craft. The most effective legal writers are those with a lively sense of craft.

Lawyers who undertake to write their own templates for document assembly systems—these will be experienced lawyers—are custom-making their own forms. Once they take the time and trouble to learn how to make the template, they presumably will be willing to continue to review and revise it to make it even more effective.

When Not to Use a Form

In simple matters, forms work fine, if they are the right forms. But even if a matter might be handled effectively by a form, it will be important to ask whether it needs to be handled at all. Today, forms for creating a living trust are offered free by financial advisors who hope to end up with the financial management of the estate. A best-selling package calls these "loving" trusts—a deft way of increasing their appeal. The forms work well enough for small estates and only a few beneficiaries. But a great many of the people who execute do-it-yourself living trusts don't need one.

In more complicated matters, people who try to avoid legal expense by using forms can get into real trouble. So can lawyers. Some of the people who consult lawyers are inclined to view all lawyers as experts in all fields—and some lawyers may be inclined to agree with them. In cases where their own knowledge is insufficient, lawyers have an ethical obligation to retain experts. It would border on malpractice, for example, to attempt to handle an estate that exceeds the current Federal Estate Exemption amount, unless you have experience in QTIP trusts and understand the spousal deduction, and can deal with the argot of estate planning.

Finding experts can be tricky (A Fellow of the American College of Trust and Estate Counsel would do the trick in the case just presented). Once found, however, experts will not be more expensive in any field of law since they know what they are doing and therefore will take less time to do it.

Ask yourself also how your client will feel if the document you present appears to be a form. Printed forms can be effective if your client or the other side is likely to invest them with authority. But sometimes your client will want to see that you have given the matter a kind of special individual attention that is not revealed by the use of a form, no matter how sufficient to the task it is in legal terms.

How to Revise Forms Effectively

Forms can acquire a remarkable persistence. The redundant and opaque language in the form for a release in the 1936 formbook is repeated word-for-word in the release presented by the Wall Street lawyer yesterday. The language in the form probably dates from the 16th century. Even when they haven't been interpreted by a court, forms in agree-

I overheard a client talking in the office. "Most lawyers just cut-and-paste. Steve's stuff looks like he wrote it." Felt pretty good about that.

—Steve, a lawyer

I was consulting in a firm in Atlanta that handled large underwriting deals. A junior lawyer and I were considering a provision in a draft agreement that we agreed could be written much more clearly. He said he wasn't going to change it.

"This is a standard provision in these agreements," he said. "If I change it, the lawyer for the other party will want to know why, and we'll probably have to spend two hours talking about it."

33

ments can persist because they have become familiar to the parties. When forms have become conventional, trying to revise them can complicate matters, even if the revisions clearly "improve" the document.

If you decide to change a printed form, do not change it by interlineation. To begin with, the lengthy, single-spaced, small print contracts that are submitted with such an air of finality by the representatives of large real estate or securities brokerages will have no space for additions or other changes. Also, the company's representative is likely to regard any suggestion that the standard form be changed as blasphemy. Under these conditions, you can add to the printed contract a reference to an appendix and place in that appendix provisions which protect your client and provide that anything in the printed contract contrary to the provisions in the appendix is void. It is surprising how this little device will satisfy the parties, all of whom, once the form has been produced, are eager to close.

Forms are addressed again in the sections on Contracts (pp. 96-100) and Boilerplate (pp. 99-100) in Chapter Five, Writing for the Future.

> The forms for real estate contracts in the South and Southwest provide for a termite inspection but limit the liability of the inspector to the fee paid for inspection. Here you want an addendum saying that the seller warrants that the premises will be free from termites for a definite term.
>
> — A real estate lawyer

Checklist: Forms

- Don't let forms cause you to underestimate the importance of the practice of fact.
- Consider the sources of forms.
- Compare different versions of forms.
- Don't assume any form covers all the bases.
- In forms that list many items, beware *exclusio unius.*
- Remember that using forms from a data bank can waste time if the document is to be reviewed and negotiated.
- Consider whether improvements to a familiar document will generate unnecessary alarm in the other side and prolong negotiation.
- Remember that printed forms are sometimes seen as more trustworthy.
- Revise printed forms through addenda, not interlineation.
- Remember that some clients will not appreciate having their special matter handled by a form.

Letters

Effective Lawyers Write Effective Letters

A good letter can do more good, and a bad letter can do more harm, than documents that seem much more substantial. Good letters get things done. Bad letters generate more letters, more delay, more litigation—more trouble for the lawyer and expense to the client. Most new lawyers underestimate the importance of letters and what it takes to write one that is effective.

Law students and members of the public might assume that when lawyers are not in court they busy themselves writing briefs, pleadings, and motions. But most lawyers, even litigation specialists, spend a very large part of their time writing letters—to clients, other lawyers, banks, title insurance companies, and others. Many successful lawyers never write a brief or read one during their entire careers.

Lawyers are known by their letters. Because of their importance, your letters deserve as much attention as you can give them. No letter should go out without having been revised at least once in hard copy.

Effective Letter Writers Know Precisely What They Want a Letter to DO

To write an effective letter, lawyers need to develop a precise idea of what they want each letter to accomplish and tailor the contents of the letter toward that end, with the reader kept constantly in mind.

To do this, lawyers will need to push their thinking about their purposes to a level beyond what is customary. A lawyer may say to herself that she is writing "to inform the client" about how a matter is proceeding. But a lawyer's purpose in writing a letter is almost never merely to inform the reader. When lawyers inform readers, they do so to *induce an attitude*—for example, to keep clients happy with the progress of the case—*or an action*—for example, to get someone to accept an offer, pay a bill, agree to a stipulation, or both. Letters supply information only to accomplish this larger purpose.

Only when lawyers have a clear understanding of a letter's purposes are they in a position to know how to write an effective letter. Let's say a lawyer is writing a letter to another lawyer to get her to stipulate that she will not oppose a motion to lift a stay in bankruptcy, so that a sale can take place that would benefit the recipient's client. The letter will not be effective unless it makes clear how the recipient will benefit from agreeing to the request not to oppose the motion.

Letters from lawyers are often ineffective because they don't make their purpose clear and don't relate the matter in the letter clearly to that purpose.

Effective Letter Writers Imagine the Situations of the Reader

The situation of the lawyer or client who receives your letter is probably like your own. Your letter is one in a pile of other mail. Affairs are pressing. Deadlines are imminent. Taking up each letter in the pile, the recipient asks:

> *Do I need to read this? Now? Am I being asked to respond? Now? When? What is it I'm being asked to do? Why?*

If your reader cannot answer these questions at the end of the first several lines of the letter, you are in trouble. Letters that make clear their purpose right away are more likely to generate an immediate response. If letters aren't read and responded to when they are received, it isn't clear when they will be read and responded to.

Letters to lay persons need to be sensitive to the emotional world in which the letter will be read. Lay persons usually do read the letters they get from lawyers. But these letters may be read in a cloud of high emotion.

Knowing your reader well can make some letters harder, not easier, to write. We imagine only too vividly how our good friend is going to take the bad news we have to convey. In such cases, it can help to get someone who is more detached to write or read the letter, if this is an option. It is usually best to convey bad news up front in any case. It is almost impossible to conceal the fact that bad news is coming, and readers will skip to find out what it is anyway.

General Guidelines for Letters

Keep Letters Short. One-page letters are probably read all the way through four times as often and with twice as much understanding as letters that are longer than two pages. It often takes longer to write an effective one-page letter than it would to write a less effective three-pager. But readers appreciate the difference. You can't always limit a letter to one page, but you can do it more often than you think.

For letters that have to be longer than a page, it is even more important that the letter's purpose and the desired response be made clear to the reader in the first one or two paragraphs. Longer letters should provide on the first page a guide to the contents that permits the reader to skip around to find the important parts. This guide can be provided in the form of a list or in a paragraph that sets out the items in the order in which they appear later.

Consider separating out portions of potentially long letters and attaching them in appendices, as did this lawyer:

> *Dear Veronica:*
>
> *I'm enclosing a series of charts summarizing my analysis of the documents listed in our recent Requests for Admission. At this point, the charts may be useful primarily to identify the witnesses necessary we need to list in our final Disclosure Statement. The summaries require some explanations, however...*

Sears was my client. The judge's opinion said, "Developing this policy is a formidable task but certainly not beyond the skill and competence of Sears." I didn't have to read any further: I knew I'd lost that round.

—A trial lawyer

You need to keep in mind not only your immediate reader but the larger audience your letters may have when information copies are distributed.

—A senior partner

Mark Twain once wrote to a correspondent, "I apologize for the length of this letter. If I had had more time, it would have been shorter."

The following tips help you keep letters short and may increase their effectiveness in other ways:

- If you attach copies of letters or other documents referred to, the recipient has no excuse to ask someone to get them out of the files.

- Demands need not be repeated if they are part of the enclosed letters.

- When someone fails to answer your letter, direct the next letter to someone, anyone, with more authority than the person who failed to answer.

Here is a letter to another attorney that gets a lot done, and gracefully, in a small space.

> *Dear Arnold:*
>
> *Here is an Offer of Judgment for $3000 plus costs. I have looked at this file again, and I still can't see where your client is coming from on the damage issue; his medical records just don't support the idea that he was treating for the accident. Is one of the doctors going to say otherwise?*
>
> *Even if your client does not accept the Offer, I don't think the facts suggest that the claim is worth anywhere near $30,000. Shouldn't this be in compulsory arbitration? The cost of taking it to jury doesn't seem worth it to either of us. If your client will not authorize you to stipulate to transfer, I think that the facts are clear enough to allow me to file a motion.*
>
> *Please let me hear from you.*
>
> *Sincerely,*

- The Offer is made firm by being enclosed.

- The lawyer's client, not the lawyer, is identified as the source of the difficulty.

- The basis for rejecting the plaintiff's claim for damages is made clear (though not too clear) and is asserted without animus.

- Facts may be developed by the question about the possible testimony of a doctor, a question hard to ignore as asked.

- The consequence of rejecting the Offer is made clear, again without animus, so that the lawyer's cooperation in stipulating to a transfer to arbitration can be requested.

Here is a one-page letter written by an associate and two revised versions produced by a senior attorney. The first revision attempted to work from the associate's draft. The second revision started over in an attempt to make the letter even more effective.

Associate's version:

Carlton Allred, Esq.

Leonine, Falconry and Chase, etc.

> *Re: Your Client: Orange Limited Partnership*

> *My Client: Diane Divine*

Dear Carl:

> *Having spoken to Harvey Zinn, Esq., Mrs. Divine's personal attorney, it is my understanding that at this point you might be willing to stipulate to not opposing my motion to Lift the Stay before the Bankruptcy Court. As you know, any and all declarations which I plan to utilize at the hearing must be filed by November 17th.*

> *With that in mind, I would like to prevent the expense of an appraisal report; if you would agree to signing the above-referenced Stipulation, that should obviously be done sometime in the next couple of days so that the Stipulation may be filed immediately with the Court.*

> *I also understand from my conversation with*

Mr. Zinn that once you stipulate to lift your opposition to our Motion, if my Motion is granted by Judge Olson and Mrs. Divine in fact receives a deed of trust for the property, that would open up communication between yourself and Mr. Zinn regarding the possible negotiation of the sale of the property to your clients.

I would appreciate your prompt attention to this matter simply because time is of the essence; I look forward to a response from you by mid-week. If I have not been able to procure a signed Stipulation by then, I will proceed to obtain a Declaration and we will at that point presumably proceed to hearing.

Sincerely,

Senior lawyer's rewrite of Associate's draft:

Carlton Allred, etc.

Re: Jones Bankruptcy, your file #

Dear Carl:

Mr. Zinn, my client's personal attorney, suggests that you might stipulate to my motion to lift the stay in the Bankruptcy Court. Lifting the stay would prevent the expense of an appraisal. I enclose a proposed form of stipulation. I must file by November 17th.

I also understand from Mr. Zinn that if my motion is granted by the judge and my client forecloses, you might wish to communicate with Mr. Zinn regarding the possible sale of the property to your clients.

Sincerely,

Second rewrite by senior lawyer:

Dear Carl:

I enclose a proposed stipulation to lift the Stay in this matter so that Mrs. Divine can obtain good title to the property by foreclosure of her deed of trust and sell it to your client at a price to be negotiated.

Please sign and return the Stipulation if it meets your approval. If not please telephone me so I can prepare for the hearing, which is set for November 17th.

Sincerely,

Be Alert to Tone. Letters convey information not just about legal matters but about the writer of the letter. This information can be more important than the "legal" contents. Since letters written to other lawyers can't be put into evidence, they are sometimes written in less guarded ways. Remember: your opponents will reach conclusions about the quality of the opposition from your letters.

Typographical errors or poor formatting will *not* be overlooked by the usual recipients of a lawyer's letters—a judge, a court, an adverse lawyer, a co-counsel, or most important, a client. A well-written, typo-free, and professionally prepared letter creates credibility. "Minor" imperfections can have highly adverse effects.

Personal letters are more effective than form letters. Consider adding a handwritten note to standard form letters—the letter that explains to clients how a claim stemming from a car accident is to be pursued, for example.

All too often lawyers write as if they were engaged in a rote exercise. Remember: you are writing to a person, someone who doesn't like being treated like an object any more than you do. On the other hand, you should avoid the merely chatty in letters, especially at the beginning and at any length. Even in letters to friends, a chatty tone detracts from the professional quality needed for effective letters.

Wait a Day to Reply to Any Letter.

"_____ you. Strong letter follows."

We recommend that you wait 24 hours before deciding to mail *any* letter, *especially one written in a hurry, in irritation, or in high emotion.* This is harder than it seems. If you are tempted to send off a reply right away, make yourself show it to a colleague. The more important the communi-

---

The shortest letter we have seen to date is the following one:

Ed Watrous
700 Park Avenue
New York, N. Y.
Re: Your Letter of September 2.

Dear Ed:

No.

Sincerely,

After a couple of letters, I know what kind of lawyer I'm up against.

—A trial lawyer

---

cation—if it is a negotiation letter, for example—the
important it is get a check on yourself.

Fax machines and email have been a boon to litig
because they generate the immediate and impulsive
Like letters, fax messages cannot be recalled once ser
edited for improvement. They can surface at inconve
times. What is sent off in haste is often repented at lei

The temptation to write clever and insulting rejoi
can be hard to resist. To help themselves clear their m
some lawyers find it helpful write angry and sarcastic l
they have no intention of sending. They do this be
know they aren't thinking straight, no matter how ins
they feel. Some letters are most effective when left i
drawer. Lawyers who write such letters on word pr
sors should be careful, however, that these missives d
remain in the file, where they can be subpoenaed, and
been.

Don't Sneer and Don't Threaten. The tone of your
tells your reader how you are imagining your relatic
them. *Effective legal writing does not question the good
or intelligence of the reader.* A snide, righteous, or cc
scending tone is never effective in legal writing, espe
in letters. It is surprisingly hard to avoid such a tone.
is a list of oh-so-easy-to-use expressions whose tone
inevitably put readers off:

> *Is it actually your contention that*
> *You cannot really believe*
> *Do you actually mean*
> *You appear to think that*
> *No one could conscientiously contend*
> *We question the wisdom of*
> *I wish to inform you*
> *We would have you know*
> *You evidently misunderstood*
> *You seem to be confused*
> *If you will reread my previous letter, you will see*
> *I do not intend to*
> *We do not see fit to*

Most lawyers have found letters in the file that have caused them to exclaim, "My God. Did I say that?"

—A senior partner

The 18th century poet and lexicographer Samuel Johnson gave this famous advice to revisers: "Read over your compositions, and when you come to something that strikes you as particularly fine, strike it out."

Your neglect
Although you assert that
We cannot understand
Your insinuation
If this is the case
Do let us have

If you will read drafts of your letter aloud trying to imagine yourself in the place of your reader, you may be able to catch infelicities like these. They are not effective legal writing, even in cases where you fully intend to take the recipient to court.

Do not threaten the reader. Threats drive lay people into the arms of lawyers and cause lawyers to head for the courthouse. Avoid words like *sue, seize, enforce,* and *take action.* Euphemism and indirection can do much to preserve the spirit of accommodation and compromise, as in "*My client is very concerned . . . ,*" or "*My client would like to dispose of the matter before the end of the accounting year . . . ,*" or "*My client's creditors demand . . . .*" Debtors should be addressed in courteous and even sympathetic terms. Their blood pressure will have gone up thirty points anyway on seeing a lawyer's letterhead.

Never threaten unless you have the power to enforce the threat *and* you AND your client intend to follow through. The consequences you are threatening should be clearly set out. Do not allude generally to "*dire consequences.*" Say specifically what will happen and when, and when the time comes, do it. It is all right to let the reader hear a little thunder in the West, as in

> *You may wish to discuss the possibility of adjusting this claim without resort to litigation. If so, I would be glad to talk with you.*

or

> *My clients will then review their options, some of which appear to be quite favorable* [The reader is supposed to wonder, Which ones?] *and will act accordingly.*

I was a new lawyer and negotiating with one who'd been around a while.

"I guess we'll have to go to trial," said I.

"Oh, goody," said he. "That's how I make my living!"

or

> *I write this letter because it appears that litigation may be instituted in which I will have to establish the facts recited above.*

Some opponents or debtors will be obstinate and refuse or stall discussions. A remarkably effective device in such a case is to draft a complaint and send it to the opponent or debtor, perhaps with a comment to the effect that since it appears a court will have to decide the controversy the attached draft will clarify some issues in advance.

When you yourself receive a threatening or insulting letter, NEVER respond to it the same day and never in kind. Generally, the more abusive your opponent's letter, the more calm and polite should be the reply.

How to Induce a Response: A Summary

- Keep letters short.

- Say what you want early in the letter and again at the end.

- Don't threaten.

- Include a polite deadline—for example, one dictated by the requirements of a third party.

It can also help to

- Enclose papers to be signed.

- Follow up with a telephone call, which you may promise in the letter.

- Ask the client to furnish information or perform factual research: this involves them in the case.

I once received an insulting letter that I simply returned without comment. What could the writer do? Send it back? Write a worse one? Calm down?

He calmed down, and the case was settled.

—A trial lawyer.

Specific Kinds of Letters

In this section:
The Client Letter
The Evaluation Letter
Correspondence with Other Lawyers and with
Non-Lawyers

Technical Letters
Title Opinions
Estoppel Letters
Opinions of Counsel

The Client Letter

The first letter to the client should be the one that confirms the terms of the attorney-client relationship. Malpractice insurers strongly recommend these letters. Firms may have a form, but the forms should be carefully customized. In these letters:

- Confirm the *limitations* on the lawyer's undertakings, like whether the lawyer has the responsibility to pursue an appeal or the duty to file tax forms. It should not set out limitations that haven't been discussed in advance.

- Confirm discussion of *fees and expenses*. The letter can specify a range and promise to let the client know before fees and expenses are allowed to exceed a specified amount.

- *Estimate time* needed for performance.

- *Explain that telephone calls might not be returned as promptly as you both might wish* if you have to be in court. You might also introduce your staff and explain how messages are handled when received.

- *Do **not** add any terms that were not discussed and agreed to.*

Malpractice insurers also recommend that attorneys write letters to confirm that they have decided **not** to represent someone who came to them. They also recommend letters of "disengagement" at the end of a relationship to confirm admonitions given for the client's protection and to confirm who is responsible for what in the future. And they recommend setting up a procedure in the office that automatically sends to the client all written documents that pertain to the client's matter except when the lawyer decides otherwise.

In the course of your representation, write letters to your clients at every opportunity. Long delays are common in the practice of law. Clients who don't hear from the lawyer frequently assume that their matter is being ignored. It is important to handle a matter well, and it is just as important to satisfy the client that you are handling it well. Keep your clients informed, if only to explain a delay. Constant communication with clients undoubtedly reduces claims of malpractice, other considerations aside.

Regular reports can help keep your client from being alarmed at the envelope with your letterhead on it. Long complicated letters are unnecessary. Documents should be noted as "For your information—no action necessary" when appropriate to prevent undue anxiety in the client.

Confirm telephone conversations in letters to clients. This is particularly important if you have given the client advice, both to remind the client of the advice and to preclude claims that it wasn't given. It is almost impossible to go back and recount accurately the details of a telephone conversation weeks or months after the fact. Get in the habit of making notes as you talk.

Be professional, but not pompous or formulaic. Instead of writing

> *We are in receipt of yours of the 16ᵗʰ instant, the contents of which have been duly noted,*

imagine yourself talking directly with the person receiving the letter and focus on the purpose of the letter:

> *We have no objection to your . . . ,*

or

> *You are quite right to think that . . . ,*

or

> *Will you please send me. . . .*

The Evaluation Letter

In recent years, clients who are frequently in litigation — like insurance companies or large corporations — ask their attorneys to furnish them with letters from time to time that evaluate the progress of a matter. Insurance companies

---

It is often difficult to tell a prospective client that he or she has no case. But the grievance committees of Bar Associations all over the country are burdened with complaints from disappointed clients against lawyers who took poor cases.

— A federal judge

I send to the client a copy of every paper produced, even a copy of the brief.

— A senior partner

may ask the lawyer to write a letter as soon as the investigation file is received to analyze the case, report on liability, and, if liability exists, to evaluate the amount of exposure. The lawyer must evaluate the facts, the type of injury, the circumstances of the accident and any other factors the will affect a verdict. The company will rely on the letter in deciding whether the case is to be tried or compromised.

All clients and attorneys should welcome this opportunity to point out in writing the hazards, uncertainties, and expense of the litigation. Clients know better than to expect a positive or negative answer at this point. But they are entitled to a description of the hazards of the course and how you will avoid them.

These letters are an important part of the practice of lawyers who represent target defendants. They should be written in a detached manner. They should also contain an escape hatch for unexpected developments—for example, new facts that do establish liability. They should be carefully revised and edited, and are not for the inexperienced.

Correspondence with Other Lawyers and with Non-Lawyers

Correspondence with other lawyers is useful chiefly

- to confirm oral conversations

- as a memorandum

- to keep a client aware through copies that a matter is active

- to generate activity when that is needed

- to confirm important dates.

Most non-lawyers treat any letter from a lawyer as a threat, and nothing will drive a person to a lawyer or the courthouse faster than a letter that offers threats. Don't even imply a threat unless you have the power to carry it out and your client is inclined to do so.

Technical Letters

The three addressed here briefly are title opinions, estoppel letters, and opinions of counsel.

The insurance company lawyer claimed my client hadn't disclosed two previous operations, but I could produce a letter written almost a year before informing the adjuster.

—A trial lawyer

Title Opinions. Some lawyers are often called upon to give opinions as to the title of real estate, less frequently for personal property. Before title insurance companies came into existence all real estate was conveyed in reliance on an opinion of title written by a lawyer who consulted an abstractor whose business it was to locate and abstract every recorded document in the county. Today, perhaps 40% of real estate transactions are made in reliance on title opinions written by lawyers. Lawyers may rely on their own examinations of title or on title insurance policies.

Such letters frequently point out defects and make recommendations to correct them. Every defect, actual or potential, should be listed. A defect can be waived if it develops that it is waivable but it cannot be asserted after a party has relied on the title opinion to any extent.

Most readers of this book are not likely to have occasion to write such opinions. This is highly specialized field with standard provisions that have come down for centuries.

Estoppel Letters. In large transactions, a party may wish to estop another party from asserting certain matters that might emerge in the future but cannot be predicted because there is no record, or negotiations are in progress, or a decision is yet to be rendered by a court or quasi-judicial body. What is asked for here varies tremendously according to the nature of the transaction. Estoppel letters are a matter for experienced and skilled lawyers, and are not within our scope at this time.

Opinions of Counsel. In recent years, some lawyers have begun to request assurances from opposing counsel — before property will be acquired or an agreement executed — that in the opposing counsel's opinion all transactions were properly handled.

This kind of letter — for which there is apparently no other label than "opinion of counsel" — is not popular. Most lawyers refuse to write them on the grounds that they address something that the lawyers requesting the opinion ought to find out through their own efforts. Some malpractice insurers decline to cover such letters.

3 Writing through the Trial

Trial lawyers usually have good oral skills, which may or may not be matched by their skills in writing. They tend to see themselves as trench-warriors and thus to focus more upon action than upon tedious preparation of the sort they think writing calls for. But effective writing is crucial to effective litigation. The writing done through the trial sometimes shapes the trial in key ways. Writing can help a lawyer develop oral argument. As courts rely more on writing to help them clear clogged calendars, the ability to write effectively becomes even more important for trial lawyers. Some state courts now make preliminary rulings based entirely on written submissions. The losing party must then request a hearing. This discourages oral argument: can you justify to your client an expensive court appearance if it only confirms the loss?

A trial is a contest. But effective litigators always remember what clients may not realize: most civil litigation—probably over 95%—ends not in verdicts but in compromise. Effective litigators write with this in mind. This does not call for writing in a mealy-mouthed way. It calls for writing in a professional manner that makes one's points powerfully but professionally, without undue bias or hyperbole. Clients may want their lawyers to act as if they are engaged in a struggle to the death, but lawyers will serve their clients better if they conduct themselves in ways that preserve the spirit of compromise. The letters they write to their adversaries can be especially important toward this end. (See Letters, pp. 35-44)

Through the trial, many different kinds of writing are produced, with very different objectives, and for very different audiences. Some of this writing is subject to strict rules concerning content, arrangement, and length. We will note these rules and will highlight the principles of effectiveness for the various kinds of writing, which we take up in chronological order. Our focus will be on civil litigation: all references to procedures will be to the Federal Rules of Civil Procedure. More than half of the jurisdictions in the United States now use these rules, or will be using them or a version of them within the next few years.

Writing toward the Trial

In this section:
Pleadings
Discovery Papers
    Written Interrogatories
    Requests for Admission
    Requests to Produce and Inspect
    Pretrial Statements
Writing Toward Settlement
Trial Memoranda
Writing to Support Oral Argument
Trial Briefs

Pleadings

To initiate the trial, lawyers write pleadings. The pleadings allowed under the Federal Rules of Civil Procedure (Rule 7) and the rules of many states are limited and include the *complaint, answer, counterclaim,* and *reply.* Any other application to the court is called a motion.

The first rule of pleading is that you should file one only if you believe in good faith that you can make your case. This good faith belief is required by the canons of professionalism and by Rule 11 of the Federal Rules of Civil Procedure. We mention it here because it is also a criterion of effectiveness. If a judge perceives anything less than good faith, your case is doomed—and you may be subject to sanctions.

Under the rules of procedure now governing most jurisdictions, a pleading is merely a notice of a claim or defense.

Effective Writing

Rule 8 of the Federal Rules of Civil Procedure requires merely a "short and plain statement" of

- the grounds upon which the court's jurisdiction depends,

- the claim showing the pleader is entitled to relief, and

- a demand for judgment for the relief to which the pleader claims to be entitled.

The Appendix suggests a form of complaint such as:

COMPLAINT FOR MONEY LENT

1. Allegation of jurisdiction.

2. Defendant owes plaintiff _____ dollars for money lent by plaintiff to defendant on June 1, 1936.

Wherefore, plaintiff demands judgment against defendant for the sum of _____ dollars, interest and costs.

Signed: _____

Attorney for Plaintiff

Address: _____

Beginning lawyers sometimes feel an obligation to set out in some detail in the pleadings all the claims or defenses they can think of. *With notice pleading, it is unnecessary and usually unwise to go into detail.* The rule is that "[e]ach averment of a pleading shall be simple, concise, and direct." There is no danger that you will be too "short" or "plain." Amendments will always be permitted. Even during trial, amendments are permitted to conform to the evidence.

In pleadings to which a response is required, *it is important to deny any "averment" you do not wish to admit.* The Federal Rules say:

> We see in this "short and plain" statement an example of the tenacity of legalese: How else does one account for the "Wherefore" in the prayer?
> —A trial lawyer

Averments in a pleading to which a responsive pleading is required [except concerning amount of damages] are admitted when not denied in the responsive pleading.

Denials must be specific. General denials of ALL averments are possible only if they can be made in good faith.

You may *move to strike* juicy allegations of the sort that get the attention of the press, like allegations made in the early 1990s in suits filed against officers of failed savings and loan companies. But experienced litigators in the fields which generate juicy allegations rarely bother to ask the court to strike them because (a) it would result in the allegations being enthusiastically published in the press again and (b) the jury does not see the pleadings.

It is a good idea to move to strike some pleadings. If punitive damages have been claimed, and no facts pleaded could justify them, a motion to strike the claim will do no harm and may do some good.

The common law offered numerous *technical pleas* such as *demurrers, pleas in bar, motions to strike, motions to make more definite and certain, exception, bills quia timet*, and the like. The federal rules abolish these, but some are very much alive in the state courts. Such "pleas" may best be seen and handled as motions. The demurrer, for example, is the equivalent of the federal motion to dismiss for failure to state a claim.

> Juries don't read the pleadings: true. But in our court, they can "hear" complaints read. Only once in five years has a lawyer asked for this.
>
> —A state trial court judge.

Discovery Papers

In this section,
> Written Interrogatories
> Requests for Admission
> Requests to Produce and Inspect

Discovery is a major aspect of the practice of fact—the means by which a litigator develops the facts and learns what the other side is up to. No competent trial lawyer would try a case without discovery. You cannot give too much time to it. Discovery is easily subject to abuse, however, and is a major reason why litigation is so expensive.

Effective Writing

Beginning lawyers in large firms commonly find themselves having to prepare discovery papers for cases they do not know much about and probably will not try. This can be a challenge. Their difficulties are compounded by the fact that law school probably has not done much to prepare them for the practice of fact.

Under the notice system of pleading, the complaint need not tell the defendant anything except that there is a claim. Defense counsel must learn the opponent's facts by discovery, either oral or written. Plaintiffs can discover facts that help them defeat whatever defense is offered.

Discovery is also the means by which the litigator "fixes" the facts, so that witnesses may be challenged if they change their stories at trial, as they can do. If witnesses have repeated a story several times during discovery, it becomes more difficult to get away with changing it later.

Abuses of the discovery process are producing changes that will make necessary greater care in writing discovery papers. Discovery is abused either by extending it unnecessarily and adding expense to the client or by spurious objections to valid requests. New rules in many jurisdictions now limit discovery drastically. Judges are increasingly willing to sanction abuses. *Lawyers concerned about effectiveness will not abuse the process* in this way. In discovery papers, as in other court papers, judges expect good faith.

The devices of written discovery are *written interrogatories, requests for admission, and requests to produce and inspect.*

Written Interrogatories. Lawyers differ as to whether discovery should commence with the *oral deposition* of the adversary's witnesses or by *written interrogatories.*

It is easier to begin with interrogatories, especially when uniform interrogatories are used. But responses to interrogatories are always given cautiously: invariably they are prepared by the lawyer and they must be signed under oath or verified under penalty of perjury.

Many experienced trial lawyers prefer to take oral depositions from the parties and potential witnesses first, and as soon as possible. (Defendants can gain an advantage by

LITIGATORS spend too much time in discovery, turning over every rock on the beach. TRIAL LAWYERS turn a few and enter the water.

—A trial lawyer

The railroad, in a case arising out of a crossing accident, claims that the engineer had twenty years' service without an accident. The plaintiff can discover that the engineer has also had fifteen reprimands during that time. The defense then discovers that three were for his watch being slow, two were for wearing wrong shoes, three were for failure to attend meetings, and seven were for refusing to run because the track was bad.

—A trial lawyer

returning a notice of deposition with their answer; plaintiffs should give notice of depositions as soon as permitted by statute.) At this stage, the witness or party has usually not been "sandpapered" by the opposition, and the raw truth is more likely to emerge. "Impartial" witnesses, when they get into the spirit of the case by having their depositions taken, begin to root for one side or the other. Sometimes unconsciously they color the truth a bit, state it in terms most favorable to their party, or simply evade questions that they sense are harmful.

On the other hand, in an oral deposition quick-witted witnesses can sometimes elude you in a way they cannot if responding to a well-written question. In technical matters, when a particular witness for a party may not have the information you want, interrogatories enable you to find out who does. Representatives of a party can't just say "I don't know" when responding to interrogatories. They must attempt to get the requested information. *Lawyers trying to pin down witnesses in an oral deposition should be careful not to overdo it.* You may educate the opposition thereby and lose the chance for a telling cross examination at trial.

The court rules of many jurisdictions provide for *standard interrogatories* in certain kinds of matters, and sometimes require their use. These standard (or "uniform") interrogatories are used to obtain general background information that the questioner is entitled to know. They reduce paperwork.

Some states permit an unlimited number of *additional interrogatories*, though they may require lawyers to follow certain procedures if they exceed a given number. "Non-uniform" interrogatories are employed to develop the facts of the case further. These interrogatories are served like a motion or other legal paper, to be answered in thirty days and signed under oath by the party.

Do not delegate the preparation of non-uniform inter-rogatories to an inexperienced lawyer. It is too valuable an opportunity to think about strategy and too valuable an opportunity to produce information on which the whole case can turn. Interrogatories should be prepared with diligence, after thorough analysis of what the plaintiff's testimony might be, keeping in mind that the party or party's witness may be adept at avoiding harmful questions.

Questions must be drafted to exclude all possibility of equivocation. This is not easy to do, but your chances of doing so are better in written documents, where you have the opportunity to ponder and revise your question. *Each question must cover only one point.* Compound and complex questions allow witnesses to answer the question without giving you the information you want. Lawyers must be adroit and imaginative to make it difficult for witnesses to dissemble, qualify, or exaggerate.

Inexperienced lawyers tend to fear the adverse answer. But *it is much better to hear the adverse answer or learn the damaging fact early*, as the prosecution discovered in the O.J. Simpson trial. You can work on adverse matter at deposition. You can't work on it at trial.

We have said that responses to interrogatories are always given cautiously. They had better be. Witnesses who have testified in an oral deposition can refresh their recollection or realize they are mistaken, and later say so in court with candor. Lawyers cannot escape the consequences of answers written out in their own offices.

Some guidelines for responding to interrogatories:

- *Let witnesses state their answers in their own words to start with.* As with affidavits, this allows you to involve your client in the case and avoid credibility problems that creeping legalese produces.

- *Be sure not to overstate your case.* Do not let your injured client claim he can't bend over at all when on his good days he can. Sworn and written answers have a powerful effect when read to a jury.

- *Take care that your written responses are accepted by your witnesses as their own.* It doesn't help when a witness, confronted in court by an inconsistent answer on an interrogatory, says, "Oh, well, the lawyer wrote that."

- The lawyer's signature on the responses to an interrogatory means something. Under Rule 11, the signature of an attorney or party

  > constitutes a certificate by him [sic] that he has read the pleading, motion, or other paper; that to the best of his knowledge, information, and belief formed after reasonable inquiry it is well grounded in fact and is warranted by existing law or a good faith argument for the extension, modification or reversal of existing law, and that it is not interposed for any improper purpose such as to harass or to cause unnecessary delay or needless increase in the cost of litigation.

The court may impose "an appropriate sanction" for violation of this rule, which may include more than expenses.

Requests for Admission. Under Rule 36 of the Federal Rules of Civil Procedure, a party may serve on any other party a request for the admission of relevant facts.

This is a valuable tool because it is directed to the party, not the witness, and encompasses all facts in the possession of the party. In written interrogatories, a witness can use lack of knowledge as an excuse for not answering, unless they are a managing party. In responding to a Request for Admission, the party cannot deny a fact on the grounds of lack of information unless the party states "that he has made reasonable inquiry and that the information known or readily obtainable by him is insufficient to enable him to admit or deny."

Requests for admission must be drafted with even greater care than interrogatories to make a failure to answer amount to an admission.

Anything not answered is deemed admitted. Requests for Admission can be used in quasi-legal matters. If not denied or objected to, the admission will become an admission for the purposes of a pending action.

Requests to Produce and Inspect. If you are using experts, you may want to use this tool to allow the expert to examine evidence and develop the basis of the expert opinion. If the testing will be destructive, it is requested using this tool.

Pre-Trial Statements

In many jurisdictions, court rules require the parties to submit pretrial statements, at the beginning of the trial or a few days before, to prepare the judge for a pretrial conference during which the judge may wish to propose options for settlement. This is a common practice even when not required by court rule. The document does not become part of the record or go to the jury, but it must be served on counsel, who will be given time to respond.

In federal courts, the pretrial statement is a comprehensive document that sets forth the trial plan of each party, including a list of witnesses and evidence. In some state courts, the document is a joint statement that is prepared with the other party. *It is much easier to prepare if you have managed to maintain cordial relations with the opposing counsel.*

In pre-trial statements, the parties get down to the nitty-gritty—what the case is about and what is extraneous to it. *These statements should be written with no noticeable bias and without hyperbole.* This is an occasion for informing, not for persuading, the judge. Objections are made only to assist the court. Do remember: these statements can produce admissions.

> **Exhibit objections: If not made fully, the court may admit or refuse, according to its whim, and objections are waived. VI(a)(5) Uniform Rules of Practice. A very interesting rule that is infrequently followed by lawyers, with disastrous results during trial!**
>
> —A state trial court judge

Writing toward the Settlement

Before suit is filed, lawyers try in various ways to resolve matters for the benefit of their clients—through demand letters, negotiation, perhaps through mediation. After suit has been filed, but before the trial begins, lawyers will often be encouraged and sometimes be required by the court to try to settle the case in settlement conferences or mediations. Much of the work in such proceedings is done orally, but writing can help or hinder coming to terms.

For pre-trial settlement conferences and for court-ordered mediation, writing is used to set out initial positions and sometimes to take stock of where the efforts to settle have gotten so far. To write effectively in such situations, lawyers must remember whom they are trying to persuade. Writing done for a judge or arbitrator attempts to persuade a third party who is not one of the disputants. If it succeeds in persuading this third party, it is effective whether or not it persuades the other party, which it usually won't. *Writing done in efforts to achieve settlement, however, must persuade or help persuade the other party if it is to be effective.*

Since most trials are settled, lawyers should always write in ways that encourage settlement, even when they are writing to judges. This means writing in ways that make one's points clearly and forcefully but without animus and without insulting the other side. As in letters, lawyers must be alert to the tone of their writing (see pp. 35-44 and pp. 149-150).

One of the strongest inducements to settle comes from the sense that the lawyer on the other side is a worthy—and honorable—adversary. If a lawyer thinks the other lawyer is inept, or if the impulse to fight has been triggered, lawyers and their clients will pursue cases they know are weak.

It is important to show not only that you have a strong case which you are able to make strongly, but that you are fair. In papers written to the court you usually don't need to show that you are able to see things from the other party's perspective, and usually you will concede to the opponent only what you feel you must if you are not to damage your credibility with the court. But the prospects for settlement are improved when one side feels that the other side is sympathetic and reasonable. Papers written to set out your position for a settlement conference or mediation will not be seen by the judge or jury, and in them you can concede points you would not concede in court and you can acknowledge the other side's point of view. Showing some "give" can help you move toward settlement.

Not all matters can be settled, however, and you should take care not to educate the other side as to your weaknesses or strategy.

In papers written for these occasions you can address emotional, human interest issues, and bring in facts that wouldn't or couldn't be mentioned to a jury. You can also talk about what you believe the jury will do. In some ways, this writing is not different from what you do for demand letters, except that demand letters will be read by an adjuster or a committee, and settlement packages may be read by parties themselves.

In some jurisdictions, the parties will be ordered to appear before a settlement judge, who is someone different from the judge in the case to be litigated. Settlement judges typically go back and forth between parties who are kept in different rooms, carrying offers and making suggestions. Submissions to these judges are confidential, and they expect that you will offer to them a candid assessment of the weaknesses of your case, as well as the strengths.

Trial Memoranda

Trial memoranda are prepared by the lawyers, or by a skillful assistant, for their own use as a kind of road map for the course of the trial. They are similar to Pre-Trial Statements, but are written for trial counsel, not for the court. They set out the issues, provide a plan for how to handle the facts of the case, and may also provide citations to cases and statutes that are expected to be useful during the taking of evidence. *They should summarize the projected testimony of each witness and set out the order for introducing each item of evidence, and they should consider alternate courses to be taken in case of emergency.*

Writing to Support Oral Argument

Like the transcripts of song lyrics, the transcripts of effective oral arguments do not capture what makes them effective. Still, lawyers renowned for their abilities in oral argument have testified to how much they rely on writing to prepare for oral argument. They *write out complete arguments, they outline, they highlight, they search for key phrases and themes.* They make better oral presentations, they go on to say, when they "lose" the writing they have done and argue from the heart, *relying as much as they can on story, rather than abstract reasoning.* But the preparation and thought that went into the writing they "lose" is crucial. For effective oral presentations, it is just as important to do the writing as it is to "lose" it when you are actually speaking to the judge or jury.

Most law students learn in moot court or appellate argument courses that it is not a good idea to plan to read an argument you have written out. The judges will interrupt you with questions before you get very far. If you are prepared only to read through your argument and are unable to respond in a flexible way to the questions, you are in trouble. You can seem unresponsive if you seem always to be trying to get back to the outline you prepared rather than addressing the questions the judges present.

Don't read, or recite, presentations to a jury either. The jury will not interrupt you, but they won't stay with you for long. You want them to feel that you are trying to communicate with them, not that you are trying to get through a prepared presentation. With juries, the well-told story is most effective.

How can lawyers use writing to help them get ready to respond in flexible ways to questions from judges? Outlining your main points may not be enough because outlines commit you to presenting your points in a particular order. What you need is the ability to come into your argument at a particular point and move in any direction toward other points you want to make. In the section on *General Strategies for Rewriting before, during, and after Writing* (pp. 125-131), we suggest making images of your writing. To prepare for an oral presentation, something more useful than an outline might be a cluster around several focal points.

With this image in mind, you will be able to move more flexibly around through your field of argument than you would if you were committed to a linear outline.

If you are preparing to speak to a jury, the same consideration applies. You will have particular points you wish to get through in an opening or closing argument, but you don't want to appear to be making points in lockstep fashion. You want the jury to feel you are trying to communicate with them, and you want them to feel your commitment to your case, not to an argument you have prepared in advance.

After a recent hearing, while waiting for the elevator, I heard the well-known local attorney who had just appeared before me lament to one of her/his colleagues: "I had a great legal argument prepared for Anderson's court: it went straight over his head. The stupid S.O.B. kept interrupting me with his silly questions. He called "time" on me before I could finish the argument." Around the corner, stupid S.O.B. was shaking his head. The legal issues were refreshingly complex, but not difficult. Stupid S.O.B. had serious questions about the facts, though, that were still unanswered. Stupid S.O.B. reflected on how irritating he had found judicial officers' questions when he was a practitioner, and how very misguided that was.

— Wm. David Anderson, "Ten (or so) Thoughts for Domestic Relations Practitioners and Litigants," *Arizona Attorney*, Oct. 1998

You also need to be able to respond to thoughts and ideas that come to you during your own presentation—just as you would in conversation—without becoming diffuse or losing your thread. This means that you need to have a clear sense of what the "thread" is—your theory of the case. Ideally, and with the benefit of thorough preparation, you will have a clear theory before the case starts, and it won't change during the trial. You will refer to this theory as you consider whether and how to cross-examine witnesses. If a witness's testimony is damaging, but not damaging to your theory of the case, you may decide not to distract the jury by challenging the testimony.

You will be developing your theory in your motions, your discovery, and your trial memorandum (see p. 75). But note: a "theory of the case" is different from an outline of the case. *Theory* comes from the Greek root that refers to *seeing*. When you have a theory of the case, you have an image of it as much as you have a logical argument about it. This image allows you to respond more flexibly and spontaneously in your efforts to communicate with your listeners, without losing your focus.

Trial Briefs

With the permission of the court, trial briefs may be prepared, lodged with the judge, and served on opposing counsel. These briefs state what you will prove, how you hope to prove it, and the elements of the case. Where knotty evidentiary problems may arise, you may cite briefly the law applying to such problems. For example you might anticipate a hearsay objection by pointing out the exception that applies in this instance. *Trial briefs are not addressed to juries and should not argue the case.*

Judges sometimes request these briefs. Try to anticipate such requests: it is not fun to have to prepare them at night or on the weekend. Junior attorneys are often called upon to draft them.

Writing to Ask the Judge for an Order: Motions

In this section,
Pre-Trial (Dilatory) Motions
Motions for Summary Judgment
Post-Trial Motions
Other Motions
The Form of the Motion

In motions, lawyers ask the court to make particular orders before or during a trial. Motions, say the Federal rules, "shall be made in writing, shall state with particularity the grounds therefor, and shall set forth the relief or order sought." Counsel may properly communicate with the court only through motions, with notice to the opposition, except in emergencies.

The effects of motions reach beyond the particular rulings made. *The ruling on a motion can determine the shape of a whole case.* Motion practice preliminary to trial is the arena in which the legal theories of the case and tactics begin to develop. The ruling on a motion for summary judgment can conclude the case without a trial.

Your first motions in the trial introduce you to the judge who will probably be hearing the case. The impression you make with such motions can have an important effect on how things go for you later. If you are in a court where the judge who hears the early motions is not the one who will hear the trial, effective writing becomes even more important. *The writing in your motions will be what begins the work of educating the judge about the case and about what kind of a lawyer you are.* For these reasons, motions usually should be written and argued by the lawyer who is going to try the case, not delegated.

What is true about pleadings is true about motions: lawyers who wish to be effective will never file any motion or other court paper unless they fully believe in and can support their argument. *Good faith is crucial to effectiveness.* In motions, even the slightest perception that a motion is not presented in good faith will result in a quick denial. It will also taint your other dealings with that judge. "No harm,

---

Most lawyers do not prepare motions with the care and attention they deserve.

—A state trial judge

Lawyers lie in their briefs. They actually misquote the record or the case. It's so easy to catch them. All you have to do is look at the record or the opposing briefs. I sometimes thought I could let that point go and look to the rest of the argument. The other judges on the court would close the book right there.

—A state appellate court judge

no foul" does not apply if a perception of bad faith is what caused the judge to rule against you.

Trial and post-trial motions are not the occasion for hyperbole. By now the judge is familiar with the case and a smoke screen will only do harm.

Almost all courts try to deal with the blizzard of motions by designating a day of the week, usually Monday, as Law and Motion Day, or Law Day, or Hearing Day. At the beginning of the day, a great stack of files is piled on the clerk's desk. The judge is invariably pressed on these days, and conditions are not ideal for working one's way through complex arguments.

Judges may not read the whole document that has been submitted to them, particularly if it is voluminous and doesn't let the judge get quickly to what the matter is about. But it is never wise to assume that the judge hasn't read the memorandum. When in doubt, ask if the court has had an opportunity to review the submissions.

Lawyers should not rely on oral argument to clarify an unclear memorandum, no matter how good they think they are on their feet. In some courts, lawyers must now ask permission to make oral arguments of more than five minutes. And if the judge finds it necessary to rely on oral argument to make clear what the memorandum has not, you are starting in a hole of your own making. Many motions are reviewed on appeal, where they have to speak for themselves. Oral argument can't help you there.

Pre-Trial (Dilatory) Motions

A "dilatory" plea or motion is one founded on some matter of fact which is not connected with the merits of the case but that must be presented before the answer is filed or be considered waived. The permitted motions must be heard and determined before trial unless the court rules that they should be heard at trial. They are listed in the Federal Rules of Civil Procedure as

Lack of jurisdiction over the subject matter

Lack of jurisdiction over the person

> **A lawyer who deals in bad faith with a judge is done forever. Judges discuss lawyers.**
>
> —A state trial court judge

> **There's no harm in asking: "Has the court had time to review the papers?" If the answer is yes, do not recite what the judge has read. Try: "Are there any questions or concerns the court holds?"**
>
> —A state trial judge

> **I used to keep some of my zingers for oral argument. Those days are gone.**
>
> —A trial attorney

Improper venue

Insufficiency of process

Insufficiency of service of process

Failure to state a claim upon which relief can be granted

Failure to join a necessary party

Because such defenses must be disposed of before the merits are reached, they necessarily cause delay. Many lawyers employed them improperly for that purpose and "dilatory" became a derogatory term. Now, in some jurisdictions, court rules provide that a lawyer's signature upon a pleading, motion, or other paper constitutes a certificate that the paper is well-grounded in fact, that it contains a good faith argument, and that is not intended to harass or cause unnecessary delay. Courts may order sanctions for violation of the rule upon motion or upon the court's own initiative. Sanctions can require payment of the offended party's expenses, including attorney's fees.

Courts are reluctant to invoke sanctions, which can give the appearance of bias against one side. Nor does punishment of your opponent or your opponent's client itself advance your client's cause, especially if done on your demand. In motions requesting sanctions, avoid the accusatory tone. It must be clear that it is the facts, not you or your client, that demand sanctions.

Motions for Summary Judgment

The motion for summary judgment deserves special consideration. In this motion, a lawyer claims there is there is "no genuine issue as to any material fact" and "that the moving party is entitled to judgment as a matter of law." Either party may file such a motion at any time and support it by affidavits and discovery and other documents.

When a lawyer and a client feel they have a strong case and are eager to minimize delay and expense, there is an almost overwhelming temptation to move for summary judgment. This can be a mistake, especially in the early stages. *The motion educates opposing counsel as to the law and your strategy.* The court will almost always give counsel on the other side a chance to amend.

On the other hand, suppose that as you approach the trial, you make motions for summary judgment that are turned down because your opponent claims to be developing facts that will present an issue. Later on, if your opponent hasn't been able to develop what was promised by the beginning of the trial, another motion for summary judgment will have increased force.

If your motion for summary judgment is successful, you will learn that *nothing is easier to appeal from than a summary judgment.* The record is not extensive at this point, so the appeal is not expensive. Any "genuine issue" of fact will defeat a motion for summary judgment, and on review the court must view the facts in the light most favorable to the party against whom summary judgment was taken. Appellate courts seem to delight in conjuring up issues of fact to justify a reversal. Trial judges, who are not fond of being reversed, know this.

An increasing number of jurisdictions, however, are making it easier to affirm summary judgments by making the standard the same as for a directed verdict. Judges can affirm summary judgments if they conclude that no reasonable juror could find for the loser, even if a triable issue of fact is present.

Consider a partial summary judgment motion rather than risking denial of the whole motion because one facet is weak. Rule 56 encourages granting motions on the issue of liability alone although there is a genuine issue as to the amount of damages.

The strength of the motion rests entirely on facts admitted in the pleadings or presented by affidavits, depositions and discovery.

The ordinary motion is limited to the facts alleged in the pleadings. In motions for summary judgment, facts are supplied by affidavit or discovery. If the facts appear to be strong enough to justify a motion for summary judgment,

- review the case again objectively,

> A lawyer of my acquaintance used to file lawsuits at the drop of a hat and without much preparation. He expected to be educated by the motions of defense counsel. He would then attempt to plug holes in his own case as they appeared.
>
> —A trial lawyer

> If there are substantial depositions it is generally very easy for opposing counsel to show issues of fact.
>
> —A federal district court judge.

- determine where the evidence is thin,

- do the necessary discovery,

- obtain affidavits to bolster those weak places so as to pin down all the facts necessary to establish that no triable issue of fact exists.

Be generous with affidavits if you can get them, both in terms of number and length. Brevity is not a virtue in affidavits. *Facts in affidavits are accepted as true if they are not rebutted.* If you let the witnesses write out statements in their own words as the basis of the declaration, you can avoid the legalese that can affect the credibility of these documents.

Facts achieved through discovery are potentially more forceful than those established by affidavit. With affidavits, the opposing attorney can always argue the need for more discovery.

In many jurisdictions *a separate statement of facts is required* on motions for summary judgment, but even if it is not, you should provide one, just as with any other motion, and to get the court's attention, *it should be brief and clear.* Brief clear statements are not produced quickly. Expect to revise this statement more than once. Some states require that this statement of the facts refer specifically to the supporting evidence. You will need to know the supporting evidence in any case since you may be challenged to produce it. Don't fear you'll leave something out. You can amend your motion, under Rule 56, to include any facts pleaded or established through affidavits and discovery.

If at all possible, file a cross-motion. It is remarkable how many cases are decided on cross-motions for summary judgment.

When you are moving for summary judgment, you can argue also that if your motion is denied, there are facts which would prevent any summary judgment in favor of your opponent. It is important here, though, not to give an impression of weakness.

Effective Writing

Post-Trial Motions

After an unfavorable verdict, the defeated lawyer may file certain motions, such as a motion for judgment notwithstanding the verdict, or motions for *addittur* (to increase damages as a condition of denying a motion for a new trial) or *remittitur* (to diminish the amount of a jury verdict). Depending on circumstances, other motions are possible, such as a motion for a new trial because of newly discovered evidence.

When the trial has been lost, it will not be easy to maintain your composure, especially at the moment the verdict is announced. But it is better not to flinch or react. If your *post-trial motions* are to have any chance of success, they *must be written in the most professional manner possible,* with great care and respect for court and counsel. To the extent possible, *limit yourself to matters that might lead a judge to grant the motion.*

In almost all cases, the Motions-for-New-Trial contain numerous issues that will never get you any relief.

— A federal district court judge.

Other Motions

- Motion for Judgment on the Pleadings (*rarely called for, and even more rarely does it dispose of a case since the court can give leave to amend*).

- Motion for a More Definite Statement *(almost never granted because of the notice system of pleading and the right to discovery).*

- Motion to Strike *(asserted mostly by young unschooled lawyers and people arguing for themselves).*

The Federal Rules permit other motions, many of which are holdovers from common law pleading and deal principally with trial and post-trial matters. For example:

- Motions in Limine (to exclude prejudicial matter)

- Motions for Judgment Notwithstanding the Verdict

- Motions for New Trial

- Motions for New Trial on Damages Only

- Motions for Remittitur (to decrease the amount of an award)

- Motions for Additur (to increase the amount of an award)

- Motion for Enlargement of Time (many of these)

- Motion to Alter or Amend Judgment

- Motion for Leave to Amend

Motions simply ask the court to take an action, and there are as many different kinds of motions as there are ingenious litigators to conceive them and facts to foster them.

At common law, certain "writs" could be requested from the court. These ancient remedies are many and various. Still in use in federal practice are mandamus, prohibition, habeas corpus (used frequently to have witnesses made available), certiorari, and the more esoteric *quo warranto*, and *coram non judice*. Relief formerly afforded by other writs must be requested by motion. Some jurisdictions have cleared away this Latin underbrush by providing for "special actions" incorporating all of the various forms of relief which were formerly afforded by these antique procedures.

With these motions, particular care must be taken to state, clearly and concisely and not didactically, *the jurisdiction of the court* and *the facts of the case impelling the court to exercise it.*

The Form of the Motion

In state or federal courts, an effective motion will meet the requirements set out in the Federal Rules of Civil Procedure. Under rule 7b (and the rules of most states), every application to the court is presented in the form of a motion, which "shall be made in writing," shall "state with particularity" its grounds, and shall "set forth the relief or order sought."

The federal rules also require that the motions be captioned properly. The caption should have *the name of the court, title of the action, file number, and the nature of document.* The motion must be signed by counsel as a declaration of good faith under Rule 11.

At the very outset, the judge must be told the nature of the case and the facts relied upon. Judges are presumed to know

Once, in a case I'd won, we were arguing to a judge the amount of attorney fees to which we were entitled under a statute which awarded attorney fees to the winning party. The judge asked the young opposing counsel if she wanted to respond, and she did. Her response was, "Your honor, I want attorney fees too."

—A senior partner .

Our rule states, "All motions made before and after trial shall be in writing, shall indicate the precise nature of the relief requested, shall be accompanied by a memorandum indicating, as a minimum, the precise legal points, statutes and authorities relied on, citing the specific portions or pages thereof, and shall be served on the opposing parties. . . ."

—A state appellate court judge

I think judges decide motions on the facts. Mostly, they want to be fair and do the right thing. Only if the law leaves them no choice will they do otherwise.

—A trial lawyer

the law. Do not assume that they know anything about the nature and facts of your case. This is the most important part of the motion. It gives the judge the first and strongest impression of the case, and it may be determinative. The statement should include all material facts, but it should be concise as possible. It should be diligently revised, refined, and compressed. Revise this part again after you have written the whole motion. The best introductions are (re)written last. The *final version should comprise not more than ten lines*.

State the facts dispassionately even if the opposing party or counsel seems clearly in the wrong. Inflammatory language may be useful to excite a jury, but judges do not approve of counsel trying to punish each other. Just give judges the facts that allow them to conclude on their own that you deserve to prevail.

In motions, as in other written argument, it is often difficult to decide what is too much and too little. The pronouncements of handbooks don't help much. We might say to you, as we just did, "Be concise, but do not omit any material fact." But you will have to rely on your own judgment as to what is material. Counsel from colleagues should be sought when it is available.

If you argue a point of law, be precise, and present a narrow issue to the court. Do not expatiate on the law. Avoid the tone of the lecturer. Young lawyers must remember that judges, unlike law professors, are not interested in how much you know. They are interested in learning how to decide particular questions.

Motions need not be lengthy, but they must *be absolutely accurate in their citation of authority and in their statement of any facts not pleaded or admitted*. In some states, facts not pleaded or admitted cannot be used in a motion; they make it a "speaking motion," which is defective.

Take special care to be accurate in your citations to authority and to the record. You will never regain the confidence of a judge to whom you have given an incorrect citation or with whom you have been less than candid. A mis-citation is inexcusable, and usually unforgettable.

It is of course mortifying, in the root sense of the word, to rely on authority that has been overruled.

> **KISS [Keep It Simple, Stupid]! Judges are not real smart. Chart it! Cartoon it! Simplify it! Keep it short. Cite best, controlling case in your state.**
>
> —A state trial court judge

> **Invariably, exhibits are tabbed for counsel's copy—and the file copy—but not for the judge's copy. You figure it!**
>
> —A state trial court judge

> **Except in their first year on the job, I don't think there is any judge who reads motions word for word. What you always see in a judge's chambers is a highlighter and paper clips. I wonder: has anyone ever watched a judge read a motion?**
>
> —A trial lawyer

> **And unforgivable.**
>
> —A federal district court judge

> **Worse! You'll never recover.**
>
> —A state trial court judge

Unfortunately, some judges perceive brevity in written argument as a sign of indolence or lack of desire. This is a book on effective legal writing, not good legal writing, so you are advised that such judges should be accommodated with some embellishments to the argument that may not be necessary to be effective with other judges. The more perceptive judges will appreciate a concise memorandum going to the heart of the matter. Such judges will not infer thoroughness from the voluminousness of the brief or the quantity of the citations. In fact it works the other way for these judges.

Beginning lawyers usually do not know as much as they would like about the preferences of the judges before whom they are arguing. They should find out what they can. When

If you are going to move to exceed the page limit, do it first! Do not file the motion with the brief! That's arrogant, and the judge may well deny it, or say "I'll just read 'til the page limit is reached—in no particular order!"

—A state trial court judge

Voluminousness is a turn-off to most if not all of us. A four-page brief is very impressive. A twenty-five-page application to exceed the limit because "we can't do it in twenty pages" is a brief doomed from the file stamp. Why attach a 10-page document when one paragraph on one page does it! Then highlight it.

—A state trial court judge

Because of the length of their motions, they had to come from way back in oral argument. I'm not sure this is true in federal court because of the law clerks. But brevity still helps.

—A trial lawyer

Checklist: Motions

- Am I making this motion in a good faith belief that it is valid?

- Does my motion begin with a statement of the nature of the case and the pertinent facts?

- Is this statement not more than 10 lines long?

- Does it contain all the material facts, while remaining concise?

- Does it state the matter dispassionately?

- If my motion argues a point of law

    Does it keep the argument to a narrow point?

    Does it avoid lecturing the judge?

    Are citations to the law and record absolutely accurate?

- Is the relief requested in language that the judge might adopt for the order?

in doubt, give the judge the benefit of it, and assume that you are dealing with someone who will prefer conciseness.

A lawyer's reputation for thoroughness, integrity, and candor can make the difference in motion practice, as elsewhere. Beginning lawyers, who have yet to establish their reputations, are reminded that these qualities—or the absence of them—are inferred from the way you write at least as much as from any other aspect of your practice.

Conclude your motions with the language you would like to have in the court's order. You need to convince the judge not only to rule in your favor, but also to give you the order you need. Consider attaching a proposed order. Do not be greedy; do not ask for more than you are entitled to. You probably will not get the relief, and you may lead the court into error.

Writing at the End of the Trial

In this section,
Jury Instructions
Answers to Questions from the Jury
Jury Interrogatories and Special Verdicts
Post-Trial Memoranda
Form of Judgment

Jury Instructions

In cases tried to a jury, judges read instructions to the jury to tell them the law that should be applied to the facts proved. Many standard instructions now exist. One such is the instruction on burden of proof. *If standard instructions exist, the court will use them.* If there is no standard instruction, instructions are prepared by counsel for each side and submitted to the judge. Counsel then meet with the judge in chambers and argue their positions on the applicable law, or the applicability of particular law. The judge decides on the instructions to be read to the jury, which may have been redrafted by the judge.

The instructions submitted to the judge must be written in a highly professional manner, supported by appropriate citations. It does no service to a client to induce a judge to give

There is an ancient saying: "Know before whom you stand."
—A trial judge

We were before a bright, intelligent judge. There were lots of motions. It would not be an exaggeration to say that the paper from the defense was four times what we submitted. But we won 75% of the motions, even though they often had better points. And this was a judge who did read the papers.

Usually what is hoped for is a paper which complies with THE RULES!
—A state trial court

Don't ever try to lead the court into error. That is a deal killer!
—A state trial court judge

73

improper instructions. This will almost certainly work a reversal on appeal.

Judges usually know the difference between instructions that have withstood appeal and instructions that are understandable to juries. *Lawyers should not lecture judges on what would be understandable to a jury*, but they can raise the question to a judge if it might help the judge to accept the instruction proposed. The first consideration for a judge, however, is always whether giving the particular instruction would be reversible error.

In a case tried to a judge, no instructions are submitted: it is assumed that the judge already knows the law and requires no instruction. This does not foreclose legal argument to the judge.

Answers to Questions from the Jury

Juries may be instructed that they can ask questions of witnesses through the judge either during trial or after the jury has retired. These questions come in written form. Judges will often ask both counsel to submit answers and attempt to get them to agree on the phrasing.

Because the situations in the law vary so much, not much general advice can be given about drafting these answers beyond saying that they must be drafted with great care. Lawyers can let down after a case goes to the jury. *If they get a question from the jury, they need to give it their best attention.*

Jury Interrogatories and Special Verdicts

These are requests to the judge for answers to specific questions of the finder of fact concerning particular findings. The losers in the case are the ones who want this information. Judges are reluctant to grant such requests because they tend to muddy the waters. Special verdicts might be requested in criminal cases involving lesser-included offenses, where the jury can get to the lesser offense only if they fail to find guilt beyond a reasonable doubt as to the greater offense charged. In civil cases where punitive damages have been requested, counsel might want to know what actual damages were found.

The lawyer requesting the special verdict submits a proposed form of verdict, which could be accompanied by a memorandum but rarely is.

Post-Trial Memoranda

In non-jury cases, the judge will frequently take the case under advisement. Usually the court will order counsel to file legal memoranda supporting their contentions. These memoranda are not allowed unless requested by the court. Judges may order memoranda to be filed simultaneously within a particular period, or set specified times for one party to file, the other to reply, and the proponent to respond to the reply. *Post-trial memoranda may be the most important writing a lawyer does during the non-jury trial.* Here, counsel can argue the case almost as they would to a jury. They can bring up matters that they didn't know about before the trial started or that were not fully developed at trial.

The post-trial memorandum presents counsel's last chance to attack the credibility of witnesses. In the United States, appellate courts are bound to accept the decision of the trier of fact as to the credibility of witnesses and evidence, if any credible evidence whatsoever is adduced. In Canada, appellate courts can ask trial judges to specify a basis for their judgment on credibility. Witnesses do not testify on appeal in either country.

If the judge doesn't ask for these memoranda, a lawyer can ask for permission to file one. If you think your writing skills, or your opponent's, give you an advantage, it makes sense to request this permission. The request is not likely to be opposed either by the judge or opposing counsel.

Advocates should welcome this opportunity *to emphasize vital facts and make a cogent recital of the law.* Brevity is not necessarily a virtue here. Unfortunately some judges interpret brevity as showing lack of interest.

Form of Judgment

Winning counsel submits a form of judgment, to which the loser will be given an opportunity to object. This is not an occasion for blowing smoke. *Argumentative headings should not be used.*

> In six years, I can remember sending a special verdict to a jury maybe two or three times. I need to be concerned about anything that might complicate the jury's job. Anything that might complicate it will complicate it.
>
> —A state trial court judge

> In my experience, it's the better judges that require post-trial memos.
>
> —A trial lawyer

Be even-handed. If the losing party succeeds in getting the judge to modify one portion of your draft, other portions may come under fire.

Writing to Keep Clients Satisfied

During the battle of wits that constitutes litigation, it is all too easy to overlook your client.

Effective representation includes keeping the client satisfied about your representation. Toward this end, clients need to be told what is happening, what is about to happen, or what has happened—and, perhaps most important, why nothing seems to be happening. Delays are inherent in litigation. Clients often don't understand the reasons for these delays, and even if they do, they aren't happy about it. The lawyer may have gotten the continuance to serve the long-range interests of the client, but to the client it may seem that the client's eagerness to get on with the case is being ignored. (Be advised that a growing minority of judges require the client's signature on requests for continuances.)

It is especially important to keep clients informed when they are located far from the scene of the action. Clients are always nervous: if they are not kept informed, they will become actively dissatisfied. It is difficult to operate at top efficiency as a litigator when that happens. *Communicate in writing, not just on the phone.* A paper trail can be useful should a claim of malpractice arise.

Involve your client, where appropriate, in the preparation of a case, in drafting a statement for an affidavit, for example, or doing a bit of factual research. An easy way to keep clients informed is to *provide them with copies of all the papers filed in court, a summary of the results of discovery, and any correspondence related to the case.* Secretaries can be instructed to do this as a matter of course. Some clients like to be a part of the case. Some clients don't want to be bothered, or say they don't, but they should be kept informed anyway. Some clients will call you up every time you send them something. If you explain that a letter is costed at a minimum of 20 minutes, 1/3 of your hourly rate, plus postage and other expenses, your client may choose to leave you alone. There will be no complaint if the final result is good. If you think it won't be good, it is important to write a letter to let the client know this in a timely way. In direct communication with your client, be candid about the possibilities of success and failure.

Sophisticated clients, like corporations, can be expected to know more than unsophisticated clients about how things are done, and you will not have to explain to them what a "pleading" is. But even sophisticated clients do not know how the case is going until you tell them. Some request quarterly status reports. Some clients, like insurance carriers, may have particular preferences for how their attorney communicates with them. These preferences should be followed to the letter.

Remember who your client is. If your client in a personal injury case is 19-year-old Johnny, it should be Johnny with whom you communicate first, not his father. Fathers and mothers and whoever is paying the bills should, of course, also know what is going on, which they can learn by receiving copies of your correspondence with your client.

Then there is the letter litigators dread: the one than informs the client that the case has been lost or that all avenues of appeal have been exhausted. There is no way to make this a happy event. It is probably best not to beat around the bush or try to soften the blow. If you have kept your clients informed all along and been candid about the likelihood of success and failure, you have done all you can to prepare them for this moment.

> Every time my client received one of my carefully drafted letters, he would call up and demand to know just what the hell was going on.
>
> —A trial lawyer

> A client responded to one such letter from me: "I have read—through a red haze—your letter informing me of the decision of the Department of the Interior...."
>
> —A trial lawyer

4 Writing through the Appeal

A ppellate briefs constitute a small part of the writing lawyers do, whether the lawyers are generalists or specialists. When the time comes, however, the success of an appeal depends overwhelmingly on the effectiveness of the brief.

Before an effective brief can be written, lawyers must make a solid record at trial. The notice of appeal and designation of the record can also help or hinder the cause. The brief itself is different in important respects from other kinds of writing lawyers do. Writing an effective brief on appeal always requires imagination as well as much study, planning, and revision.

Making the Record

The practice of fact is important even for the appeal. An effective brief on appeal cannot be written unless there is a solid record to support it. On appeal, the court must consider only *the pleadings, the testimony of the witnesses as reflected in the court reporter's transcript, and the exhibits.* It is not supposed to consider any matters outside (or "aliunde," as the old cases say) the record.

The brief on appeal begins to stir into life when the trial judge makes the first adverse ruling. *The error must be made to appear in the written record.* Appellate courts can deal with "plain error" that hasn't been objected to at trial, but lawyers are obviously fighting an uphill battle when they have to argue that an error is plain on appeal even though the record doesn't show that it was noticed at trial.

Making an effective record requires more than lodging an objection for each error. During the trial, skilled trial lawyers will be considering in the backs of their minds how every development in the trial will look to the appellate court. They will attempt to make clear in the record the errors of the trial court. If evidence is improperly excluded, for example, it should be offered again using a different approach. If it is rejected again, the lawyer offering the evidence should make an offer of proof, which should have been prepared before trial.

The record of a case tried to a judge will be different from one tried to a jury. Evidence that would have to be excluded in a jury trial might be admissible in a non-jury trial on the theory that a judge is able to sort out irrelevant, extraneous, and prejudicial matter (such as the fact that the defendant has a large insurance policy), and disregard it. It has not been demonstrated, however, that legal training is proof against prejudice.

Experienced trial lawyers tend to believe that most of the time the most sensible verdict is likely to be arrived at by six or eight or twelve jurors. Juries can be stampeded into awarding excessive damages, most often in personal injury cases. If the jury stampedes, the judge may correct its error in the cooler moments of post-trial argument. There is no way to correct a stampeding judge, except through an expensive appeal.

There are cases where the judge is preferable as the trier of fact. In any case, lawyers need to build a solid record to support an appeal.

The Effective Notice of Appeal

The appeal commences officially with the Notice of Appeal, which is governed in federal courts by Rule 3 of the Federal Rules of Appellate Procedure. All jurisdictions have similar rules, varying in details only.

The notice must be filed by the deadline (or "timely filed," a lawyer might say). For the past century, nothing has been so absolutely jurisdictional as meeting the deadline for the notice of appeal. The only exception was the prisoner without a postage stamp. Nothing would save the lawyer who was late. The federal system now allows an extension of time for good cause, but it has to be very good cause indeed.

The Federal Rules of Appellate Procedure approve the simple form that follows for a notice of appeal:

> Notice is hereby given that C. D., defendant above named, hereby appeals to the United States Court of Appeals for the _____ Circuit (from the final judgment) (from the order (describing it)) entered in this action on the _____ day of _____.

We do not recommend using this shotgun form, however, unless your case is a weak one, or the judgment being appealed from is a single issue matter. In all other cases, lawyers should try to assist the appellate court, even at this early stage, by informing it of the precise nature and basis of the appeal.

At the end of the trial, lawyers know the issues in the case, but they know them as a potpourri. If the notice of appeal is to be effectively written, the lawyer initiating the appeal must sort out these issues and focus them. This may take thought, writing, and the advice of colleagues.

The notice should cover all the points on which the lawyer intends to rely on appeal. When making the argument on appeal, lawyers should not dilute their major points with minor ones. On the notice of appeal, however, minor points may be included without harm since they may be later waived. Waiving them may even help add emphasis to the major points. Omissions in the notice are fatal: the notice cannot be amended after the appeal period has expired. The fear that they will omit something is what disposes some lawyers to employ the shotgun approach.

I know a lawyer who regularly filed notices after five o'clock on the day they were due. He was pals with the court clerk, who would hold the door open for him and stamp his papers as timely received. I don't recommend this approach.

—A senior partner

Designating the Record

The federal rule requires the appellant to order from the reporter "a transcript of such parts of the record . . . as he deems necessary. . . ," with notice to the appellee, within ten days of filing the notice of appeal. If the appellee wants other parts added, "he shall designate additional parts." Other jurisdictions allow the appellant to designate the record at the time the brief is filed. By this time, the lawyer is likely to have a more secure sense of what parts of the record need to be designated.

Even where appellants are permitted to designate the whole record, they will almost always want to limit the facts, which can be so voluminous as to be overwhelming. Lawyers must also consider whether sending up the whole record will seem excessive to the appellate court. It may cost more to designate parts of the record, however, than it would to send it all up.

In a lengthy or complicated case, marshalling the facts is sheer drudgery. It must be done with great care since the appellate court is restricted to the record and every fact or exhibit referred to in the brief must be accurately cited to the record. Some of the work of preparing this record can be delegated to assistants, but the lawyer who is not in command of the facts of the case is courting disaster.

Designating the record for an appeal from a motion for summary judgment or partial summary judgment is much less expensive and time-consuming, a point to be considered when you are thinking about filing such a motion.

The parties can agree to a statement of the facts to be used as the record on appeal.

The Brief

The brief must be filed within a specified period after the notice of appeal. The period varies among jurisdictions.

We have addressed situations where good writing and effective writing may not be the same thing. In briefs on appeal, the writing must be good to be effective. In these briefs, lawyers write to discerning and sophisticated judges who do not have to operate under the immediate pressures of the trial. Briefs on appeal are no place to blow smoke. Nor are appellate judges likely to be impressed by your knowledge of the law or oratorical flourishes. As always, your job is to assist the court to arrive at the right decision on the issues before it.

Some lawyers specialize in writing briefs on appeal. Though they may never have stood up in a courtroom, they may be able to analyze the case more effectively for the purposes of appeal than can the lawyer who tried the case, particularly if they have had experience as a clerk in an appellate court. To the lawyer who was trial counsel, appellate court opinions can seem to refer to a case completely different from the one that was tried.

On appeal, the argument is carried primarily by the written brief. In oral argument, you may manage to remedy some of the deficiencies of your brief. Appellate judges render their decisions not immediately after oral argument, however, but after consideration and reconsideration of the brief. The gains you make in oral argument may be lost later as the court rereads your brief.

The Special Arguments on Appeal

Appellants are, by definition, the losers below. On appeal, they are not on the same footing as when the particular issue was disputed at trial. On appeal, they must show not only how an issue should now be decided but that the decision made below was wrong and not harmless. Appellees must make it just as clear that the appellate court does not have a sufficient reason to upset what was done below. Neither of these ends is achieved simply by replaying arguments made at trial. New arguments and new authorities must be brought to bear.

A key argument that may need to be made for the first time on appeal concerns *the standard of review*. In a criminal appeal, if court decides that the standard is whether the trial judge abused his or her discretion, the appellant will rarely, if ever, prevail. Appellants will want the court to consider instead whether the ruling below was clearly erroneous, or whether the review on appeal should be *de novo*. When the court decides which standard of review to apply, one or the other of the parties on appeal is going to feel the strain.

The Federal Rules of Appellate Procedure require that the argument of the brief shall address the question of standard of review, either with each issue or in a separate section.

The Parts of the Brief

> *In this section,*
> The Table of Contents
> Statement of the Issues Presented for Review
> Statement of the Case and Statement of the Facts
> The Argument
> The Conclusion

The requirements for appellate briefs are set out by Rule 28 of the Federal Rules of Appellate Procedure. If followed precisely, a brief written according to these requirements would be acceptable in any court, federal or state. Among other things, an appellant's brief "must contain, under appropriate headings and in the order indicated"

(2) a table of contents, with page references;

(3) a table of authorities — cases (alphabetically arranged), statutes, and other authorities – with references to the pages of the brief where they are cited;

(4) a jurisdictional statement;

(5) a statement of the issues presented for review;

(6) a statement of the case briefly indicating the nature of the case, the course of proceedings, and the disposition below;

(7) a statement of facts relevant to the issues submitted for review with appropriate references to the record;

(8) a summary of the argument, which must

contain a succinct, clear, and accurate statement of the arguments made in the body of the brief, and which must not merely repeat the argument headings;

(9) the argument, which must contain:

(A) appellant's contentions and the reasons for them, with citations to the authorities and parts of the record on which the appellant relies; and

(B) or each issue, a concise statement of the applicable standard of review (which may appear in the discussion of the issue or under a separate heading placed before the discussion of the issues);

(10) a short conclusion stating the precise relief sought.

The Table of Contents. The Table of Contents should set out the propositions that you are attempting to get the court to accept, not mere labels for topics you are addressing. You are trying to convince the judges to rule in your favor, and you should miss no opportunity you have to argue your points.

Well-formulated propositions are critical for the lawyer in any area of writing, and especially in the brief on appeal. It may take a while to arrive at them. Write out your propositions in different versions. Choose one that gets you started. Usually you can make more headway by revising a written statement than by trying to arrive at the final form of the proposition in your head before writing it down.

Before you decide on the final form of your propositions, draft the body of your argument. As you draft your arguments, you will discover more precisely how you want to state your propositions. Revise your propositions in the Table of Contents to make sure that your last version reflects the structure of the argument as you finally make it.

Unlike labels, propositions have a tone of voice, and you should make sure that your propositions are dignified as well as concise. They should not insult or drip sarcasm on the opposition—as in "Surely appellee would not be so presumptuous as to claim that a lease exists"—no matter how frivolous and idiotic their case seems to you. Judges prefer to decide for themselves that the claims being made them are frivolous and idiotic; they do not like to be told what to think.

The structure and emphasis of your headings implies the structure and emphasis of the argument. From your propositions, readers develop expectations about what is to follow, if only subconsciously. When your argument fulfills the expectations created by your headings, the proposition is more convincing.

If the case turns on the question of whether a lessee was estopped from denying the existence of a lease, the heading in the Table of Contents (and throughout the brief) should not be "Estoppel" but something like "The Lessee By Its Statements And Actions Is Estopped From Denying That A Lease Exists." Such "argumentative headings" should be formulated (and re-formulated) with special care and should match closely what is argued elsewhere in the brief.

Any proposition can be constructed in many different ways. The arguments in your Table of Contents should be constructed to make the emphasis fall where you want it to fall in the argument. The heading above might be rewritten in at least the following ways, depending on what facts and law you want to emphasize:

> *By Its Statements and Actions, The Lessee is Estopped* . . . emphasizes "statements and actions" that estop lessee.

> *Its Statements And Actions Estop The Lessee* . . . emphasizes "estop" more than preceding version.

> *The Lessee Cannot Deny That A Lease Exists Because It Is Estopped By Its Statements and Actions* . . . emphasizes argument that lessee "cannot deny" that the lease exists.

> *A Lease Exists Because The Lessee Is Estopped from*

Denying . . . emphasizes argument that a lease exists.

Statement of the Issues Presented for Review. The statement of the issues presented for review is critical. This segment of the brief (and the recital of facts) should be written with the greatest care and after thorough analysis of the impression it will make on the court. Properly written, it will go a long way toward winning the case before the court and staff even look at the cited authorities.

Be sure that in setting out the issues, you keep the reader aware of what you are arguing. You are not writing an even-handed scholarly treatment of the issues: you are arguing that the issues should be decided in your favor. These may be called "issues," but you should frame them as assertions, not as questions or "whether" statements. It should be "Jones is estopped from denying the existence of a lease," not "The Question is Whether Jones is Estopped from Denying...." or worse (because less focussed) "Does a lease exist?" You are arguing for particular outcomes, not exploring a question.

Writers are told not to repeat themselves, but in this situation, repetition is helpful. Your statement of the issues should repeat much of the language in your Table of Contents. You do not know for certain that your readers have read your Table of Contents. Even if they have, here you are not simply setting forth your claims, as in the Table of Contents: you are making them part of an integrated statement. This will offer the reader a slightly different perspective upon the issues, which is fine as long as the perspective is not so different that your readers can't see how they got there from the Table of Contents.

If you do produce a very different perspective when you write your statement of the issues, revise either the statement of issues or the propositions in the Table of Contents.

Effective repetition is discussed further in the section, "Rewrite Drafts for Readers" (pp. 136-137).

Statement of the Case and Statement of the Facts. *The statement of the case* "indicate[s] briefly" the nature of the case and its history in the courts below. Appellate courts

---

Do not fear repetition. Repetition is one of the laws of learning, and a brief is an effort to educate the reader to your point of view.

—A trial lawyer

need to know some background, and they need to know that the case is properly before them. But keep your statement of the case brief: it can advance your argument, but it is not the place to develop the argument.

The statement of the facts, on the other hand, presents a unique and crucial opportunity. The writing you do here is a different from anything else you do in the brief. This is the only place you get to tell a story. It can be powerfully persuasive. A well-written recital of the facts can, like a statement of the issues, go a long way toward winning your case before the court or staff even looks at the law. It should be written with the greatest of care.

*Write the final statement of facts **after** you know precisely the argument you are going to make.* The statement of facts precedes the argument, but that doesn't mean it is written first.

Do not obviously argue the facts or color them. Set out the facts in such a way that they argue for you. The judge should receive the impression that the statement of fact is full and fair—maybe just slightly slanted in favor of the narrator's point of view, which is only human.

Do not overstate or fudge the facts. Facts speak for themselves, and when someone tries to speak for them, they lose their power. If you fudge the facts, and the judge or the other side catches you at it, you will need to refer to the section on "Writing to Keep Clients Satisfied" (pp. 76-77), which tells you how to write letters to clients explaining why you lost the case.

Tell the court the material facts, and perhaps a few facts that are merely relevant (if they help set the scene). Take care not to omit any material fact and not to clutter up the recital with immaterial facts. Give a full statement, but not an exhaustive one. You lose readers when you make them wonder whether the facts you are presenting are material to the decision. Readers will skip to the argument, as we all do in such situations, to find out which are the material facts.

Do not omit "bad" facts—your client's fingerprints on the murder weapon, for example. Any bad facts omitted will appear on the first page of your opponent's reply brief. You can handle bad facts in ways that help your client without being unfair or violating your duty to the court. You can place them in unemphatic places in your argument (in the middles of paragraphs and briefs) and you can discount them by saying that they were "claimed" or asserted" by a particular witness.

Do not quibble over trivial matters. You are entitled to dispute your opponent's statement of the facts, and it is usually necessary to do so. But this requires some finesse. You don't want the court to get the impression that you are one of those lawyers who will dispute every issue, no matter how trivial.

Consider how you will refer to the parties. The federal courts discourage the use of such abstract legal designations as "appellant," "defendant/appellent" or "third party defendant/appellee." Consider using terms that specify relationships important in the story of what brought the people to court. If you refer to a party as "the employee," or "the fellow worker," your reader won't have to stop to figure out who is doing what to whom.

These relationships may be clear from the story, in which case proper names are often the best choice: "Cynthia Chavez-Feldman," "Ms. Chavez-Feldman." In a personal injury case, the use of proper names allows the plaintiff's lawyer to remind the court (without making a special point of it) that the decision on the legal issues affects a person. When you use proper names, refer to a party politely (No condescending use of "Cynthia") and unemotionally (The court will decide if Ms. Chavez-Feldman is "aggrieved"). Toward this end, we prefer to use "Mr.", "Mrs.," and "Ms." We believe that "Ms." should be used to refer to women unless their married state is relevant to the issue, or they have expressed a wish to be referred to as "Mrs."

A lawyer defending a personal injury case will want to use general nouns (the employee) that allow the court to focus on the legal issue, unless something about the person of the plaintiff argues against recovery.

Use proper names for corporations and other collectivities, abbreviating them after their first use, or using the general noun of reference ("the corporation," "the company," "the union.") Don't bother with the all-too-common interpolations "(hereinafter called 'Microsoft')." They're helpful only in the rare cases where the abbreviation or collective noun isn't obviously derived from the proper name.

For multiple parties, develop a proper name. Do not revert to the status designations we have been urged to avoid—"appellants," "third-party defendant/appellee," etc.

Checklist: Statement of the Facts

- Finish the statement of facts after you know precisely the argument you are going to make.

- Do not obviously argue the facts or color them.

- Do not overstate or fudge the facts.

- Tell the court the material facts, and perhaps a few facts that are merely relevant (if they help set the scene).

- Do not omit "bad" facts

- Do not quibble over trivial matters.

- Consider how you will refer to the parties.

The Argument. *Do not write as if you are simply out to "prove" your points.* To be effective, lawyers must remember that their position is that of an officer of the court who has the duty of assisting the court to do justice. You cannot do this by being pompous, pretentious, or didactic. You are there to help the judge decide the case. Remember: a court can be reversed, but it is never "wrong."

Provide a summary before the actual argument, without fail. Like everything else, this summary should be drafted with the greatest of care—only more so. Your reader encounters your argument here for the first time, and if the judge hearing your oral argument is a little behind, it may be the only part of the brief that is read before hearing oral argument.

Do not start your argument by repeating the argument of the other side. You might put it better than they did.

Don't list legal principles the court should know. Young lawyers, by reciting as they would in class, can appear to be lecturing or "talking down" to the court instead of "looking up" to it with an attitude of respect and humility. If you think the court ignorant of the applicable law, find ways of introducing it in passing that don't talk down. In general, follow the principle that the court knows the law but needs to be informed of the facts. In most cases, your strongest argument should be presented first, followed by the others in order of descending importance. Your "strongest" argument may be the one that you judge most likely to defeat the strongest argument of the opposition, or it may be one that the opposition has not dealt with. There is no formula to tell a lawyer which argument is the strongest. A lawyer must make this judgment with reference to everything involved in the case, including who the opponent is and who is hearing the case.

You will have a good sense of the issues in the case itself by the time you are finished with the trial, but these *issues must be precisely focussed on appeal.* A good device for achieving this focus is the syllogism. *Try to understand your argument as a syllogism.* The syllogism is a logical form of argument in which the conclusion (the decision you seek) is shown to derive from the application of a major premise (the legal principle) to a minor premise (the circumstances of this case). To produce a syllogism, you need to be able to state

1) the legal principle

2) the facts of the case that bring it under the legal principle and

3) the decision that is compelled by applying the principle to the circumstances of the case.

When you can grasp your argument in the form of a syllogism, you have achieved a clarity and succinctness that will take you a long way in writing the various parts of the brief and in prevailing on appeal. Notice, however, that in setting these arguments forth in the brief, the logical form of the syllogism might not put the matter most effectively.

Effective Writing

At this point it is usually best to begin with the conclusion, as in the second example below.

Compare

> *This complaint in a breach of contract action fails to allege performance or excuse for a non-performance by the plaintiff, and is therefore insufficient to state a cause of action.*

with

> *This complaint in a breach of contract action is insufficient to state a cause of action because it fails to allege performance or excuse for non-performance by the plaintiff.*

One state appellate court adopted the practice of giving lawyers drafts of opinions before oral argument. This may diminish the importance of oral argument for the winner. It makes oral argument much more important for the projected loser, who will also be in the uncomfortable position of wondering if he can justify an expensive appearance if the result is only to confirm the loss. In either case, the practice of offering tentative decisions on the basis of the briefs makes obvious the critical importance of the effectively written brief.

Consider carefully whether minor issues should be omitted. Should all the issues be argued (in the brief or orally) even though it may not be possible to devote much space or time to them? Arguing minor issues may dilute the force of the major issue. No formula will decide such questions. The best we can do is to point out the choice that must be made. In making this choice, lawyers must use all their imagination, expertise, and knowledge of the situation—and their intuition. Some advocates brief the minor issues, but argue only the main one or two in oral argument. This precludes any claim that you waived the minor issues.

Be thorough but do not write exhaustive scholarly treatments of legal issues. You are arguing for particular outcomes. Here again you must walk a tightrope between what is too much and what is too little.

> **The key is simplicity. I always do better if I can break it down into baby steps.**
> —An appeals attorney

> **Finding the syllogism is another of the parts of writing the brief that is fun. When you do find it, the brief practically writes itself.**
> —An appeals attorney

> **Too many lawyers start writing the brief before asking what lies at the core of the appeal. When you produce the syllogism, you have gotten to the core.**

> **You've got the judge's attention for about five minutes. I want to be sure that they at least understand the argument. When I put it in the form of a syllogism I can be pretty sure that they do. Whether they agree or not is another matter.**
> —An appeals attorney

> **I'm sure giving out drafts of the opinions beforehand helped us clear our clogged calendar, but some judges were reluctant to do this when they knew that cases might be settled.**
> —A state appellate court judge

91

A court will sometimes decide a case on an issue you feel was minor. The opinion may even suggest that you overlooked its importance. Judges have law clerks, and law clerks come out of law school having been rewarded for three years for finding issues that others overlook. They may approach briefs in the same spirit. Lawyers who have spent years thinking about a case can find the suggestion that they overlooked something more than a little irritating.

—A trial lawyer

Nothing is easier to distinguish than an AmJur cite.

—A trial lawyer

Judges have law clerks, whom they use in different ways. Lawyers can't tell what difference a clerk makes, since lawyers don't know the clerk, or what relationship the clerk has with the judge. This uncertainty can be frustrating, and "the law clerk" is often blamed for a less-than-satisfactory decision (as the losing lawyer sees it) by a judge. The best policy is to forget about the clerk. It is still the judge who decides.

Be absolutely accurate and complete in your use of authority. When you submit a brief, you represent to the court that every citation to fact or law is absolutely accurate and complete, and every argument is candid and made in good faith. The judge should be able to open the brief in the expectation that it will not be necessary to refer to the record or the library (unless opposing counsel challenges your veracity). If you do make a mistake, don't try to bluff the court: it is better to be considered stupid than untrustworthy.

Do not use strings of citations. The computer makes it hard to resist these. You may think that a string of citations provides more support than the citation of one case. Judges are convinced when the facts and law of particular controlling cases are clearly set out in discussion; they are not convinced by strings of citations to cases that may or may not be applicable. Don't forget what happens when you encounter such litter in the argument of an opponent. You look for the controlling case in this jurisdiction, and then see if you can distinguish it on its facts. Judges and their clerks do the same.

If none of the cases in a string is controlling, cite the first case and the most recent one, or the first case and the case in the string that is most like the one you are trying.

Lawyers don't find controlling cases as often as they would like. When you don't have controlling cases, you must consider what the court will find persuasive. We learn a hierarchy in law school. In a state court, decisions by the state supreme court are best. Decisions by the federal circuit court in one's own circuit are also likely to be persuasive. Decisions by another state's courts are more dicey. It is said that state courts in the West are not automatically inclined to defer to state courts in the East. The state courts in the

---

Checklist: Arguments

- Do not write as if you are simply out to "prove" your points.
- Provide a summary before the actual argument.
- Do not start your argument by repeating the argument of the other side.
- Don't list legal principles the court should know.
- Focus issues precisely on appeal.
- Try to understand your argument as a syllogism
- Consider carefully whether minor issues should be omitted.
- Be thorough but do not write exhaustive scholarly treatments of legal issues.
- Be absolutely accurate and complete in your use of authority.
- If a case is worth citing, it's worth quoting.
- Quote phrases, clauses, sentences.

East no doubt return the favor. But the hierarchy is not rigid, and lawyers may be able to get some mileage out of strong decisions wherever they may be found.

If a case is worth citing, it's worth quoting. Never paraphrase a court's decision instead of quoting it. This gives the reader the choice of accepting your version of the case or going to the library to verify the accuracy of your paraphrase. Woe to you if the reader reads the case and interprets the passage less favorably than you. If you have quoted the key language and candidly set forth the background, judges will be less likely to think you disingenuous, even if they don't agree with the law propounded.

Quote phrases, clauses, sentences. A paragraph, maybe. It is almost never advisable to quote more than a paragraph. Readers simply skip over block quotations (as you know from your own experience as a reader), and look to what follows to tell them what in that hunk of quoted language they need to pay attention to, if anything.

Lawyers may be reluctant to quote phrases and clauses because they aren't sure how to punctuate such quotations.

The conventions of quotation are well established and it isn't hard to learn them. Knowledge of these conventions can produce a very large pay-off in writing effective legal argument. We deal further with the art of effective citation and quotation in the section, Rewrite Drafts for Readers, pp. 162-168.

The Conclusion. *State precisely the relief you seek.* The Federal Rules of Appellate Procedure provide that conclusions shall be "short," and so they should be in practice before any court. The conclusion should not restate your arguments. Your statement of "the precise relief sought" should not appear to be telling the judge what to do. It should be written as if written by the judge, *using the precise words you would have the judge use in the order.* No one can be sure what goes on in the mind of a judge writing an opinion, but we feel there is always, and properly so, some doubt in the mind of a good judge. Judges who have decided a case might hesitate concerning the language of the final ruling. If you have offered language the court can adopt, you may have placed the final straw on the back of the opposition.

The Appellee's Brief

By Rule 28, the structure of the appellee's brief shall conform to that of the appellent's brief except that the appellees don't have to include any sections that seem satisfactory to them in appellant's brief. You will find that you are rarely satisfied with the opposite party's version of the facts or law. If the appellant's omission is a major one, amounting to a misrepresentation of the facts, land on it with all four feet. But *do not quibble over minor matters.*

You must supply omissions or run the risk of being taken to have admitted the facts as stated by your opponent. *Do not simply list omissions. Restate the facts, as simply as possible.*

Even if the rules do not require it, *conclude, as appellant does, with a statement of what you want the court to rule.* Use the precise language you think the court might use.

The Reply Brief

The Federal Rules of Appellate Procedure say only that the appellant "may" file a reply brief. The rules of some courts add that the reply "shall be confined strictly to points urged in appellee's brief." In most jurisdictions, reply briefs are filed without exception.

The contents of the Reply Brief depend entirely on the brief by the appellee. In jurisdictions where the reply is not confined to the points urged in appellee's brief, you have an opportunity to repeat your key arguments briefly. But it had better be brief. It is crucial in any case not to let any offensive move by the appellee go by default, even if it seems to you not worthy of a reply.

A number of cases mentioned in the notes to FRAP Rule 28 uphold a fifty-page limit to briefs on appeal and call lawyers on various attempts to evade the limit by incorporating trial memoranda by reference or adding a raft of footnotes. One court denied costs on appeal to a prevailing party that had exceeded the limit. We agree that fifty pages ought to be plenty.

> I once ignored an affidavit that was utterly ridiculous. The court took the material as admitted. I won't do that again.
>
> —A trial lawyer

5 Writing for the Future: Contracts and Wills and Trusts

The Memorandum of Contract

A lawyer we knew who was a very good writer referred to a written contract as a "memorandum of contract." His expression reminds us that the "contract" a lawyer writes offers only the traces of the actual contract.

Every day, many contracts are made and never "reduced" to writing. When we drive into a service station, we offer to pay the operator the listed price for gasoline, and the operator contracts that the gasoline is of merchantable quality. If we come in for repair services, we offer to pay a reasonable amount for the services, and the operator contracts that the services will be rendered by a mechanic skilled for the task at hand and that any parts purchased will be suitable for the purpose for which they are intended.

The terms of such contracts are not established by any agreement the parties sign. They reside in the common and statutory law. We would not think of presenting the station owner with a "contract" to sign before we bought the gasoline. If we did, he would probably run us off.

The Spirit of the Effective Contract

To write effective contracts, lawyers must keep in mind this larger idea of contract. What is written in a memorandum of contract is important, but focusing too narrowly on the writing can lead to ineffective contract making.

Effective Writing

Rarely can a lawyer dare to tell a client to rely on a handshake. For one thing, the hand that is shaken may not be the hand that is going to be bound to perform under the contract. But contracts can be written in such a way as to preserve the spirit of the handshake. Not many are. All too many contracts, particularly if they have achieved the dubious status of the "standard" or "form" contract, simply try to cover all the possibilities (in such a way as to favor whoever has developed the "standard" contract, of course). Such contracts become less and less understandable and less and less like a handshake as lawyers learn about the possibilities that Form I (or Form XXI) failed to cover.

The most effective contract is the one that both sides fulfill without resort to the courts. The more you and your client feel compelled to pin the other party down, the less advisable it may be to enter the contract with that party. It is better for your client to have a contract with a good person and no written agreement than it is to have a good written agreement with a bad person. Lawyers can't provide clients with good people with whom to make contracts, but they can increase the likelihood of performance in other ways.

Contracts are more likely to be performed when the parties to the contract are clear about what is being agreed to. You encourage performance more with clarity than you do with legalistic language that promises to be enforceable according to your client's wishes. People who don't want to perform may be told by their lawyers that the courts will enforce a boilerplate provision against them. But if they want to bad enough, they can find a way to make enforcement a less than satisfactory solution for the other party.

Clear understandings of the sort that increase the likelihood of performance are not produced by spelling out every last thing. They are produced by being precise sometimes and imprecise at other times. They are produced principally by telling a story in an orderly way, saying that I do this and you do that, and if perhaps certain events occur, we'll do things in this different way.

Overwriting contracts usually occurs not from negligence or omission but from misplaced zeal, uncertainty, a desire to cover all the bases, or a desire to impress the

> If I give you my hand on it, I will fulfill the spirit of the contract to its fullest, if we write it down I will do only what the words say I must do.
>
> —A purveyor of barber supplies

> It would be interesting to see which business transactions succeed best: those based on a handshake or those based on complex written agreements.
>
> —A senior partner

I once wrote a two-page lease for a lessor. The lessee's lawyer countered with twenty pages of boilerplate, which I rejected. The lessee's lawyer was indignant. He said, "You've got to negotiate." I told him, "My lease is fair and complete and I'm not going to charge my client for analyzing all your surplusage. Take it or leave it."

His client took it, the lease worked out perfectly, and the lawyer didn't speak to me for ten years.

—A senior partner

Lawyers always write much more than the business people have thought about. I've often thought that we ought to set out first the five points the parties have actually agreed to and then add everything the lawyers went on to worry about. I think this would help in interpreting the document later.

—A commercial real

client. The rococo language that results is usually harmless in strictly legal terms but it can lead to serious problems by appearing to exclude what it does not specifically include, under the doctrine of *expressio unius*.

When Is a Contract Needed?

We think about reducing an agreement to writing (or "writing a contract") when it is important to make an uncertain future more predictable—when the contract extends over a long time, or when the services sought are specialized or complicated, or when a lot of money is involved. Sometimes, we must write a contract even if we don't think we need one because of a statutory requirement or because the bank won't lend money without a contract.

People may enter into contracts hoping to make an uncertain future more predictable, but if they (or their lawyers) are not careful, they can find that they have entered contracts when they didn't intend to, or that the language they agreed to be bound by has had effects different from those they intended.

When clients ask their lawyers to draw up a contract, they are likely to feel that its terms are clear and simple. (They also may feel that they need the contract yesterday.) They consult their lawyers because something tells them that all may not be as simple as it seems. The lawyers never disappoint them. Clients are by no means always grateful for having their lives complicated in this way.

We speak of "reducing" contracts to writing, but what we actually do when we write one is expand our awareness of the contingencies that might arise and of the provisions that will govern them.

Remember Who Reads Contracts

To write an effective contract, lawyers need to keep in mind who will read them and what they will look for. Contracts are read by clients, by the lawyers on the other side, and, if they fail to be performed, by judges. Most clients will be gratified to read contracts that are brief and to the point. Some clients may want contracts that appear to govern every possible contingency.

Opposing counsel may prefer lengthy, redundant and antique provisions to clear and simple English because they have seen them before and know they have in some way passed muster. In such cases, a lawyer substituting clearer, more concise but unfamiliar words would be most imprudent.

If the contract fails in the first test of its effectiveness—performance by both parties—a judge may read it, and *lawyers do well to ask themselves how the contracts they are writing would appear to a judge.* Judges may not like boilerplate any more than lay people do. If a contract is written in such an over-reaching way as to motivate a judge to look for a way to let someone escape from its terms, lawyers may be able to take small consolation in how "tightly" they thought they had bound that person.

All these readers—the parties, counsel, and judges—will be gratified if they can move around in the document efficiently to locate particular sections that may be of interest. This means that *in all but the simplest instruments a Table of Contents should be provided* and headings used. There's possible benefit for the writer here too: developing a Table of Contents can help the drafter to organize the material better.

The memorandum should be as self-contained as possible so that the parties do not need to go elsewhere to determine their rights and responsibilities. If material necessary for this purpose is too bulky to be integrated into the body, it can be attached as an appendix. If it is too bulky to be attached as an appendix (like the specifications for most construction projects), it can be incorporated by reference.

Technical terms should be defined either at the beginning of the document or where they are used.

On the Use of Boilerplate and Printed Forms

Boilerplate. Partly to make clients feel secure, it has become customary, even in uncomplicated transactions, to try to include in a contract everything that could conceivably happen (and many things that could not). This sort of document has become much easier to produce with the advent of the word processor and computer memory banks.

> In shopping center leases the temptation is to try to think of everything, but this can get you in trouble. One lease called for all the tenants to stay open until 10 in the evening. Only one lessee was actually doing this. He sued to force the other tenants to stay open.
>
> —A real estate lawyer

While lawyers have a duty to advise their clients about potential problems they may foresee, they should not conceive of their duty in writing contracts as nailing down every contingency. It is impossible to cover every contingency, and lawyers who try to do so may vitiate the spirit of agreement between the parties by too much quibbling over details. They may also run afoul of the rule of interpretation called *expressio unius est exclusio alterius*, which holds that when a document lists items in detail, it is presumed that any omissions from the list are intentional.

A rule of thumb: The more writing you need, the greater the possibility that this isn't a contract your client should enter.

Some boilerplate provisions become so conventional that departing from them will disturb the other side. In such a case, it would be imprudent to change the provision just to make it better writing. Boilerplate is discussed further in the section, Rewrite Drafts for Readers, pp. 162-168.

Printed Forms. Many memoranda of contract are offered today as printed forms. Contracts to buy cars, brokerage contracts, credit card agreements, insurance contracts and many leases take this form. Surprising provisions can be found in them, like the provision in many brokerage contracts that allows the brokerage firm to use your stock as collateral for loans it takes in its own name.

It is apparent that some of these documents have scant claim to represent the actual contract between the parties, even if both have signed a provision saying that they have "read and understood" the memorandum. Courts have disregarded the provisions of such forms and discovered the actual contract in what the parties were entitled to expect.

Lawyers receiving printed forms from the other side may want to consider changes but they may also have to consider whether their client would be best served by spending the time necessary to change everything that needs changing. How to make changes in printed forms is discussed in the section on Forms, pp. 28-34.

I knew a lawyer who would sometimes draft his proposed memoranda to look like printed forms. He was sure—and I expect he was right—that recipients of the proposals would be less likely to suggest changes if they thought it was a printed form. I've known people who have signed printed forms involving millions of dollars without reading them.

—A lawyer

Contracts That Are Too Effective

The lawyer whose client is in a strong bargaining position or who wishes to use a printed form must remember that a contract can be too effective.

The common law of contract holds that if persons of ordinary intelligence execute instruments, they are presumed to have read the instruments and are bound by their terms. But the same law has come to recognize the deficiencies of contracts that are entered into by parties whose unequal bargaining positions make it unlikely that the contracts reflect an actual willingness to be bound by the language of the instrument. Writers of contracts must recognize that contracts may be unenforceable even when mutual assent exists, fraud is absent, and the contract has been entered into in good faith.

Courts have sometimes invented ambiguity to avoid enforcing the terms of contracts that have "adhesive" qualities. They have refused to enforce terms that they find not to have been actually "dickered," or terms that violated the "intent" of the contract or the "reasonable expectations" of the party against whom the contract was being enforced.

The contract of adhesion has long been unenforceable. A rule of law is now emerging which will relieve a party from clauses in an agreement which, in the words of one court, "he did not negotiate, probably did not read and probably would not have understood had he read them." This rule applies to boilerplate whether it emerges from a word processor's memory bank or the print shop and applies whether the contract in question is an insurance policy, a broker's agreement, or some other "lengthy and

A young lawyer showed me a letter he'd written reviewing a lease submitted by a middle management employee of a large corporation. The letter was 22 pages long and discussed in minute detail every clause of a one-year lease with a monthly rental of $1,000. The young lawyer had devoted 12 hours to the project. A week later he came back with a letter from the employee of the corporation praising the lease extravagantly and complimenting highly the counsel who had been so diligent. Of course the employee was not paying the bill.

—A senior partner

A broker's agreement currently in use provides deep in the body of the instrument that "all securities and other property may be pledged and repledged by the broker from time to time, without notice to the owner of the securities and property . . . for any amount due in my accounts, or for any greater amount." This language appears in tiny print deep within a document printed on a sheet of flimsy paper that is larger than legal size. It is fair to assume that many of the people who have signed this contract—and many have—have done so without knowledge of this language and that they would not have agreed to its terms if they had examined and discussed it.

Lawyers, or lay people, who don't like such provisions may simply strike them out. Brokers may consider it unpatriotic to question their printed form, but if the account is large enough, they will swallow their objections.

Such provisions are likely to be unenforceable even if they aren't stricken.

—A senior partner

forbidding document." A California court has stated that a standardized printed contract insurance policy is totally different from a traditional agreement reached by the bargaining of the parties.

Few lawyers will shed tears because their client's bargaining position is a strong one. But lawyers for such clients should be aware that contracts or provisions in contracts written for such clients may be unenforceable even if the client is dealing in the best of faith. The problem is not addressed by blanket provisions that ask the disadvantaged party to declare that they "have read and understood the provisions of this contract."

We suggest that lawyers writing contracts for clients in strong bargaining positions set forth explicitly the benefits to the weaker party of provisions that seem to benefit the stronger party. It may also help to negate specifically any "expectations" that they don't want a court to find later to be "reasonable expectations" and thus part of the terms of the contract.

Do not overreach. If a court finds one provision unconscionable, it will view the rest of the contract with a jaundiced eye.

How to Develop the Memorandum of Contract

Since contracts are agreements between humans, no two are exactly alike, even if the printed form that has been signed is the same. In every case, you are producing a memorandum of contract for a particular client and a particular situation.

Begin by sitting down with the client to find out as much as you can about the situation. Don't play smart: if it's a construction contract, let the client educate you about the steps in constructing the building. Even if you know how this client has built other buildings, find out how this one is to be built.

You must find out what the client considers important. But you can't narrow your inquiry to this only. From a lawyer's point of view, the most important piece of information may be something the client considers irrelevant, like the fact that the person on the other side is her brother-in-law.

I think it works best when you can get both parties in the same room and listen to them talk about why they want this agreement and respond to your questions. You can get a one-sided version if you talk only to your client.

—A senior partner

Before drafting any memorandum, you should set out clearly for yourself the context for this agreement—the parties, the purpose, the benefits, the issues.

Before starting to draft a memorandum of agreement, make a list of the principal points. Lawyers cannot limit themselves to the immediate terms necessary to reach agreement. Your function is to put into legal and enforceable form the wishes of your client.

Your client may not have thought the matter through. It is not your function to advise the client, great as the temptation might be, on the business aspects of the agreement. Lawyers who try to restrain enthusiastic clients run the risk of being accused of meddling in business affairs. If the transaction is not consummated, the lawyer may be blamed. But to serve your client properly, you must anticipate—and urge your client to anticipate—changed circumstances in the future.

Even if the terms of the contract are clear and agreeable to the parties, the lawyer's work is not done until the client has been asked to consider

- consequences of disagreement between the parties,

- what will happen if a party dies or if the economy declines, and

- what will happen if the contract is assigned.

A client may think that the best contract is one that runs to many pages of boilerplate that will pin the other parties to the wall if they don't perform. But it is impossible to nail everything down in a memorandum of agreement, given the nature of language and human ingenuity. The meaning of language is always arguable, as adolescents demonstrate to their parents every day.

If you are going to go into detail, you had better go all the way. You may consult formbooks or forms from the firm's data bank as a checklist. But do not trust the forms to catch everything you need to include. Provisions like "including but not restricted to" may appear to protect you from the dangers of the *expressio unius* rule. But such provisions are ambiguous, and may give the impression of

> **If you set out the context well, the contract writes itself.**
>
> —A commercial real estate lawyer

Once a young man who had come into riches as a professional athlete left word at my office that he wanted to make an appointment to have a partnership agreement drawn up. No detail.There is no quicker way to part a rich young man from his money that for him to enter into a partnership agreement with the wrong person. I spent several hours trying to get in touch with him to warn him not to make any commitments in advance. By the time I located him, he had, fortunately, changed his mind.

The line between business and legal advice is not always clear.

—A senior partner

overreaching. We have no magic bullet, but it may help to insert an accommodating provision like "The parties agree that there may be matters which shall become material and relevant and which have not been specifically mentioned. These will be governed by the rules of equity and the practices of the profession."

It is tempting not to spell out too precisely the obligations of your own client. Lawyers can do this subconsciously, which is understandable, but it is not effective legal writing because of the common law rule that ambiguities are to be resolved against the writer or the party offering the ambiguous instrument.

Be sure you define important terms.

The contract said "less intervening credits." We got into court because no one agreed on what "intervening credits" were.

—A senior partner

Should You Keep Drafts?

After the memorandum is signed, some lawyers destroy all drafts on the grounds that the signed document is the only admissible evidence of the agreement under the parol evidence rule. Other lawyers keep drafts for possible use in tracing the history of a dispute in the future. Some keep them only for a year, in the belief that the disputes they might help resolve will arise within that time. Lawyers will have to use their judgment about this and consider whether the storage costs justify keeping the drafts.

When people are feeling friendly, they may not be inclined to suggest changes in a proposed contract. Afraid they'll poison the well. I've found it amazing, though, how often people will just accept the changes I've proposed without batting an eye.

—A lawyer

Writing and Negotiating

Strategy in negotiation is often determined more by the personalities of the people involved than by the legal or factual issues. The more lawyers know about the other parties, the better is their position in negotiation. If, as often happens, the client consults the lawyer only after negotiation is substantially complete, the options are, of course, limited.

If you can, it is usually best to produce the first draft of the memorandum of agreement yourself so that the negotiations will proceed from your client's position. Remember, though, that to arrive at a written contract, it is necessary not only to write the instrument but to get the parties to sign it. For this reason also, it is important not to over-reach.

When you receive a draft produced by the other side, you will need to decide if it is better to analyze it or start over.

When you set out to analyze a draft, you will need to read the whole thing for general impression and completeness. Before you can do this, you will need to make sure you are up on the law governing the situation. This can call for a little or a lot of legal research, depending on your familiarity with the situation and the complexity of the transaction.

Next read the draft clause by clause, making notes on

- what is wrong with it,

- what is unclear (remembering that the other side has probably left it that way for a reason),

> Years ago, I represented a jeweler negotiating to lease a prestigious location 40' by 100' in a shopping mall. He brought me the landlord's proposed lease, seventy-seven pages in all. I glanced through it long enough to see that it contained, among other things, provisions against storing baled hay and prohibiting use of the premises for a "gasoline filling station."
>
> I handed it back to the client and said, "Go ahead and sign it. Probably nothing will go wrong and the landlord needs you more than you need him. If I charge you for the time I will have to spend in reviewing this so that I can give you a sound legal opinion and then for negotiating with the SOB that represents the landlord, you will be outraged and find another lawyer." I was right. As instructed, I did review the lease, I did negotiate with the landlord's unreasonable lawyer (I did not negotiate the baled hay or filling station clauses for I felt there was little danger that my jeweler client would engage in those businesses in a space 40' by 100'). I charged the client accordingly. I never saw him again.
>
> —A senior partner

- what should be drawn to your client's attention even if it is clear and nothing is wrong with it.

When you have objections, you have several options. You can send the draft back (a move likely to vitiate the contract, which may be just what you would advise your client to do). You can ask questions in letters, which can become part of the contract. Or you can recommend specific changes—deletions, substitutions, additions. Note: It helps readers if all drafts circulated to the client and counsel are dated and the new language is presented along with the language it modifies, with a line through the old language.

It is easier to add something than it is to take it out. If I want to strike language in which I agree to operate my motorcycle "in a reasonable and prudent manner," you may wonder why, even if I tell you that the language is unnecessary given my duties under the common law of torts.

If you are drafting a document yourself, you may wish to use the word "sell" rather than the conventional "bargain, assign, set over, transfer, and convey" that appears in the form from the form bank. If you receive a draft from the other side with the form's language in it, you may decide that the better part of valor is to let it go rather than suggest that it be made simpler and more readable.

Lawyers looking over proffered contracts soon learn that ambiguous language is not there by accident, especially when the language appears on a printed form or is part of a document offered by a party in a strong bargaining position, or an insurance company. Usually, it is preferable to remove any ambiguities you notice before executing the contract, even if it seems obvious that a court would not interpret them against your client. Weeks, months, or years of litigation can be avoided by clarifying matters at the beginning.

Particular Provisions

Essential terms in almost all contracts are

- the names of the parties,
- the nature of the business to be carried on,
- the intent,
- the undertakings of the parties—together or separate,
- the term of the contract and
- how it will be terminated.

Give some attention to how you formulate *the intentions of the parties*. This language is important in interpreting the other language in the memorandum, and it can help to tie amendments to the original document.

Provisions governing notice (where to be given, when effective) are almost always important also. Depending on the nature of the contract, it may also be necessary to address the division of profits and technical organization. In our opinion, it is preferable not to range across the contractual universe but to leave unlikely or unique matters to the rules of evidence, the common law and the applicable statutes.

Keep Some Terms Flexible. It is common to provide for insurance, for example, but a contract made in 1970 requiring one party to furnish $100,000 of insurance would be hopelessly inadequate today. Changes in amounts can sometimes be built in by, for example, tying them to the Consumer Price Index or some other recognized standard.

Do Not Use Terms That Produce Questions of Fact. A provision that obligates a lessee to operate a vehicle in "a reasonable and prudent manner," for example, is an invitation to involve the trier of fact.

Specify Consideration. We learned in law school that contracts must have consideration to be enforceable. The doctrine is alive and well, even though the Uniform Commercial Code specifies some contracts that are enforceable without consideration. The writer of a contract should spell out the facts amounting to consideration so that parol evidence will not be required to prove the existence of consideration. This is not accomplished by the common clause that reads ". . . for Ten Dollars and other valuable considerations. . . ." Be specific. If you find it difficult to specify consideration, you have been alerted to a problem with the enforceability of the contract.

Address the Possibility of Assignment. People making a contract may assume that they will always be dealing under the contract with the person or company with whom they are currently dealing. But every contract is assignable, at least to some extent, regardless of its provisions. An assignment of the contract or its proceeds is worked by death, bankruptcy, guardianship, execution, and garnishment. Even a personal services contract, which cannot be strictly enforced, can be encumbered to some extent. Assignment can be voluntary or involuntary. Every contract should contemplate the possibility of assignment to someone unpalatable to your client. The effective writer of contracts will try to anticipate the conditions for assignment and will include in the contract provisions that will control assignment to the extent possible.

A provision frequently used in an attempt to control assignment is "This contract shall not be assigned without the consent of [the other party], which shall not be unreasonably withheld." Another possible provision is "Any assignment of this agreement shall be void in the absence of prior written consent." It's a little better but probably not strictly enforceable.

It is not a good idea to agree to a contract made with "buyer, or nominee," or with a title or escrow company or some other trustee for an unnamed beneficiary. Assignment of a contract does not necessarily relieve the assigner, however, and a contract to sell to "buyer or nominee" does not necessarily bind both parties equally. The language should state clearly that the buyer remains bound after the nominee is identified, and that the nominee is bound to perform all the terms of the contract.

Consider Whether to Provide for Attorney's Fees. A provision for attorney's fees can help discourage breach or litigation. However, if one party demands to be paid attorney's fees when there is litigation, the other is entitled to ask for them. This provision might constitute an invitation to both parties to sue, because in the heat of battle, each expects to win. Overall, it does seem to help to include a clause for attorney fees. Strangely, in a great many cases the existence of provision for attorney's fees seems to discourage the stronger rather than the weaker party, perhaps because the weaker party has less to lose.

Consider Arbitration, Mediation, Alternative Dispute Resolution. We recommend considering for every contract a provision for arbitration under the rules of the American Arbitration Association or the Uniform Rules for Procedure for Arbitration, which are readily available and have complete and explicit procedures.

Many states have statutes providing for compulsory arbitration of cases involving less than a certain amount.

One client who signed a contract to "nominee" discovered to his sorrow that the nominee-purchaser had just emerged empty-handed from four years in bankruptcy.

—A senior partner

Some unhappy contracts are made with buyers who turn out to be unable to perform, especially if the seller has been offered more than the property is worth. A corporation once agreed to pay a million dollars for a property with the deed to run to the buyer corporation "or nominee" as the buyer. It is perfectly appropriate and usually prudent to require from any person who will end up being the obligee in the contract to furnish a certified financial statement.

—A senior partner

Voluntary arbitration clauses also discourage traditional litigation. Clients sometimes are reluctant to discuss arbitration at the time the contract is made. They are euphoric about the deal they are about to make with the nice person across the table and dislike even to discuss the dissolution of the relationship. Inserting such provisions is important to effective contract writing, although your client may not appreciate the service you have rendered.

Arbitration may be binding or subject to appeal. Unless the arbitrator's decision is binding, not much is accomplished; the arbitration clause may merely delay the trip to the courthouse. The method for appointing the arbitrator must be carefully and explicitly set out. The contract should also provide that the arbitration hearing shall be held within a specified time from the demand, and that the arbitrator must render a decision within a specified time after the hearing.

Other methods of resolving disputes between contracting parties are coming into use, because of the expense of litigation and delays resulting from crowded court calendars. Provisions should be considered to allow the parties to settle their controversy by other Alternative Dispute Resolution (ADR) procedures such as mediation, mini-trial or private trial. All can result in a relatively inexpensive, prompt, publicity-free, and sometimes amicable settlement of the controversy.

Be Careful with Provisions Calling for Forfeitures and Penalties. It is not immoral or unethical to provide that a party shall forfeit money or property upon failure to perform a contract, and such a provision is enforceable if the penalty is to compensate the injured party for damages in an amount which the parties have agreed upon beforehand.

But forfeitures and penalties are not favored by the law. "Penalty" connotes punishment. If a party agrees to pay a stipulated sum on breach of contract regardless of the damage sustained, the court will generally find the clause void and limit recovery to actual damages. The effective legal writer will find ways to spell out the detriment to his client of breach by the other party.

Checklist: Particular Provisions

- Keep Certain Terms Flexible

- Do Not Use Terms That Produce Questions of Fact

- Specify Consideration

- Address the Possibility of Assignment

- Consider Whether to Provide for Attorney's Fees

- Consider Arbitration, Mediation, Alternative Dispute Resolution

- Be Careful With Provisions Calling for Forfeitures and Penalties

---

Some Special Cases

Documents Organizing a Corporation. Articles of Incorporation constitute a contract between the corporation and its shareholders. They should be simple to the point of being terse and should follow closely the state statute on corporate organization. They need contain little more than the name of the corporation, its duration, and the purpose for which it is organized.

The Model Business Corporation Act is an excellent guide for the drafting of the charter, even in states where the Act has not yet been adopted. The Delaware statute startles with its simplicity. It provides (Sec. 2.02):

The Articles of Incorporation must set forth:

(1) a corporate name for the corporation that satisfies the requirements of section 4.01;

(2) the number of shares the corporation is authorized to issue;

(3) the street address of the corporation's initial registered office, and name of its initial registered agent at that office; and

(4) the name and address of each incorporator.

The Articles of Incorporation may set forth:

(1) the names and addresses of the individuals who are to serve as the initial directors;

(2) provisions not inconsistent with law regarding:

(i) the purpose or purposes for which the corporation is organized;

(ii) managing the business and regulating the affairs of the corporation;

(iii) defining, regulating and limiting the powers of the corporation, its board of directors, and shareholders;

(iv) a par value for authorized shares or classes of shares;

(v) the imposition of personal liability on shareholders for the debts of the corporation to a specified extent and upon specified conditions; and

(vi) any provision that under this Act is required or permitted to be set forth in the bylaws.

Bylaws are the ordinances of the corporation built on the foundation of the articles and should go into detail according to the nature of the proposed business. Bylaws can readily be amended or deleted, subject to ratification by the shareholders—as the Bylaws themselves should provide. Details can therefore be plentiful.

The corporation will have periodic meetings, evidenced by corporate minutes, which should be prepared by a competent corporate lawyer who will keep in mind that the actions reflected by the minutes at the moment may be examined by opposing interests months or years later.

Of particular importance is the maintenance of records to keep in existence a board of directors and officers: the occasion may come when the corporation needs to act quickly, and it cannot do this without duly elected officers and directors. The Model Act provides for such emergencies.

Security offerings are usually made by corporations, but this is a highly specialized and tricky business, and a lawyer who is not a specialist in all current tax and security regulations should steer clear of stock offerings. Malpractice insurance companies charge their highest premiums for lawyers in the securities business.

Letter of Intent and Option to Purchase. Two apparently harmless but dangerous business arrangements are the "letter of intent" and the "option to purchase" or other implied unilateral contract. Of the two, the letter of intent is the more treacherous. By its terms it does not bind the writer, but acceptance of the letter is very likely to bind the recipient, especially if further negotiations take place.

Example: I give you a letter saying it is my intent to buy your million dollar office building. You know, or, as a business person, are presumed to know, that I am trying to arrange financing, or paying architects to examine the building, or incurring other expenses. May I sell the building to someone else? With a better offer? With a lesser offer? When may I sell? Tomorrow? Next month? In a reasonable time (that is, whatever a jury may determine)?

A kind of relationship has been established the ramifications of which should be carefully analyzed. It is evident that the burden is on the recipient of the letter, with none on the sender. If your client receives such a letter, it may be advisable to reply clarifying the terms or better still, with a draft contract for signature by the writer of the letter of intent when he follows through. Your client will resist either approach and will argue that such action will discourage the writer, who has all the best motives (which is probably true) and that he may lose a deal which he'd like to make. Regardless of the motives or intentions, a letter of intent is a fishing expedition, the fish being the addressee.

Many successful business transactions have been initiated by a letter of intent, which does not detract from what we have said.

Options to purchase have most of the disadvantages of the letter of intent, except that the subject of the option must definitely be taken off the market. The contract the parties will sign if the option is exercised should always be attached to the option. And the optionee should pay for the option, even if the payment is to be credited on the sale price.

You will find that, for some inexplicable reason, even sophisticated business persons don't hesitate to grant an option to purchase especially when a lessee asks for it. If you represent a lessee, always ask for such an option if you can get it free.

Title Insurance and Warranties in Deeds. Real estate transactions cannot be done without title insurance but lawyers should be aware of its limitations and

- obtain a warranty from the grantor in addition to the policy

- avoid giving a warranty if your client is the grantor. Tell the lawyer on the other side, unless he owns this book, that he should be satisfied with that great big Owner's Policy, for which your client is generously paying the premium.

Fire, casualty, windstorm and other such insurance is intended to insure against the risk of unexpected occurrences. The premiums are allegedly calculated by actuaries (some say it is more a matter of what the consumer will pay) based on the anticipated frequency of the expected accidents.

Title insurance is different. Companies will not insure title if they are aware of any risk at all. And they may insure only against matters of record in the office of the recorder or the tax collector. Their insurance does not cover pending court cases, inchoate liens like materialmen's liens, the improper location of your improvements, zoning, or the foreclosure of a prior mortgage, unless they failed to except these in their policy. Companies may require that they be paid on the gross amount of the transaction, regardless of their insured's equity in the property, or whether they had insured the same title a month earlier. Title insurance is not assignable. There can be a question whether the company could back up its policies. Next time you see a title policy which bears the name of a nationally known title company, examine it. You will probably see that it is actually issued by a subsidiary corporation in the state, with assets of the minimum required by state law.

It is evident that John Doe's warranty in Deed A, assuming he can back it up financially, may be worth more than the title insurance policy he will give Richard Roe, even assuming the title company can back up its policy.

Two Deeds
Deed A

> *I hereby convey [property] to Richard Roe and warrant title.*

> *s/ John Doe.*

Deed B

> *For and in consideration of the sum of Ten ($10) Dollars in hand paid, receipt whereof is hereby acknowledged, I, John Doe, hereinafter called Grantor, do hereby bargain, sell, assign, demise, grant and convey to Richard Roe, hereinafter called Grantee, all my right, title and interest in and to the following described real estate: [description] together with all rights and heriditaments thereto, and the appurtenances, all and singular.*

Deed A is inartistic, but it contains a warranty of title superior to that contained in any title insurance policy.

Deed B is sonorous, but it does not contain a warranty—the use of "convey" excludes the warranty.

Deed B is an excellent illustration of the fact that legal writing contains many provisions which are not only unintelligible, but the rationale for which has long since been forgotten. Deed B is no exaggeration. At this moment, there is probably being recorded in the office of your Recorder

(Prothonotary in Pennsylvania) a deed closely resembling Deed B. Obviously we think A is the better deed. But B may be more effective because Richard Roe, and maybe his lawyer, will feel more comfortable with the impressive language, especially if the lawyer uses a form excreted from a computer memory which has digested a form from a form book. If you are fond of heriditaments, Deed B is for your client.

The Acknowledgment and the Jurat. These actions are the only two that are performed by a notary public in the United States (In other countries, the notary public has substantial powers and duties). Both actions are now lumped together under the unhappy term "notarization," and are largely ceremonial.

There is a distinction between the two, however, that can have legal consequences.

Acknowledgments. A notary public takes the acknowledgment of a party that he has signed an instrument. This can be done at the time of signing or later. If it is done afterwards, most state statutes require the acknowledgment to be formalized by a notary who is acquainted with the party making the acknowledgment. This requirement is largely ignored.

Jurats. In a jurat, a person swears to the truth of an affidavit or other document requiring verification. We would surmise that half of the verified pleadings found in court nowadays could be rejected because they do not have a jurat. The jurat has become an appendage like the whale's legs.

Even more meaningless, in legal terms, is the "notarization" that is automatically attached to a contract or other document by the person in the office who has a notary seal. The ceremony is harmless, however, and may give some satisfaction to the client.

Wills and Trusts

In this section,
Effectiveness of Printed Forms

Discovering the Client's Intent
Keep a Record of Your Reasons for Recommending
    Action
Keep Up with the Client
Style in Wills and Trusts

Of comfort let no man speak!
Let's talk of graves, of worms, and epitaphs,
Make dust our paper, and with rainy eyes
Write sorrow on the bosom of the earth.
Let's choose executors, and talk of wills.

       —William Shakespeare, Richard II

Effectiveness of Printed Forms

People don't like to think about their own death. Most people don't have wills. Even most lawyers don't.

Concern about the fate of incompetent children can prompt someone to make a will or trust, as can a family feud. Not surprisingly, though, wills are often written in emergencies, after a car accident, perhaps, or with the client in rapid decline. This can present a problem for a legal writer. In such circumstances, printed forms can be useful not because they are superior to what the knowledgeable lawyer might write in half an hour or so but because clients put more trust in printed forms.

Printed forms for trusts and estates are offered in popular publications as a way of not having to deal with and pay lawyers. Lawyers have always had to deal with the public perception—which has unfortunately sometimes been justified—that they generate work for themselves, especially in this area.

But lawyers—even those who could do better than the form does with one hand tied behind them—would do well to have printed forms on hand for the reason that clients repose more trust in them. Lawyers may be able to satisfy a client better by offering a form—which they can alter to meet the client's needs—than by composing a document themselves.

I once had to defend—with substantial discomfort—a case where a notary public in another city accepted the acknowledgment of a person who had allegedly signed a mortgage, and another case where a notary appended a jurat to a deed in a state where the law provided that deeds could not be recorded unless they were "acknowledged."

—A senior partner

I always try to be courteous. I remember hearing about a lawyer who was called by a new client who said, "I want a will, and I'll tell you exactly how to do it. I've already discussed it with my barber."

Lawyer: "And what kind of stupid advice did he give you?"

Client: "He advised me to see you."

—A specialist in estate planning

It's a shame that the Bar has left it up to the commercial publishers to produce a simple form for the cases for which it would be adequate.

—A lawyer

"Living" trusts have found favor recently as a way of avoiding probate. When they work, they work fine. But there are situations when probate smoothes the road for those who remain behind.

If you know what you are doing, you can write a will for most people in two or three pages. But people can get very serious when they have to think about their wills and they have a greater sense of security if they have a lengthy formal document to deal with their death, even if most of it is unintelligible to them.

"If you know what you are doing. . . ."—there's the rub. The drafting of trusts and wills except of the most basic kind is not recommended to lawyers learning the field on their own. Probate and trust lawyers are bound to hoary old principles of law and obscure tax laws and regulations that are changing all the time. They are expressed in language that is especially unintelligible but must be used as is. In matters of any complexity, you should refer the matter to a Member of the American College of Trust and Estate Council.

Discovering the Client's Intent

When a client comes to you to make a will or trust, discovering the client's intent is the first step in writing. This can be a particular problem if the client's competency is questionable. But even when competency is not a question, and even in non-emergencies, discovering the client's intent may not be a straightforward matter.

When you speak with a client who wants to write a will or trust, you will ask about matters the client may not have considered, and you will pose eventualities. The client can get impatient with this. Clients can have certain preoccupations, certain specific demands that create problems. They may, for example, have a sentimental attachment to a large chunk of stock that ought to be diversified.

It is usually a good idea to send the client away with an assignment to do some research and respond in writing to questions you set out. This can provide time for the client to think about matters you have raised.

A single man called to ask the cost of a Living Trust Agreement. I quoted a fee. He asked the fee for a married couple, and I quoted a slightly higher fee. He preferred the latter. I asked when he was planning to be married. He said, "Oh, I don't know. I don't even have a girlfriend, but I figure I'll get married someday." I had to pass on that one.

—A specialist in estate planning

After I talk with someone, I sometimes refer them to an attorney who is better qualified to handle the problem. I typically say that they can mention that they spoke with me. They typically say, "OK. What's your name again?"

—A lawyer

Achieving a client's intent may not be the same thing as satisfying the client. A law clerk once expressed frustration to her supervising partner after another long lunch with an old client who suggested yet another change to a trust document the clerk had worked long and hard to get into "final form."

"I thought we had agreed at that last four-hour lunch on what he wanted."

"You should understand," the supervising partner explained, "that our client is not going to sign anything we draw up. If he did, he would have to relinquish control of his company, and he isn't ready to do that. He pays us well, and we do good work for him. That is what happens here, for the present."

—A junior partner

Keep a Record of Your Reasons for Recommending Actions

When you are establishing trusts for clients, you may recommend courses of action—like diversifying a block of stock that will go into the trust—that the client follows but that, through the vagaries of the market, do not turn out well for the trust. You may also recommend courses of action that the client declines to follow that do turn out to have been in the best interests of the trust. You should therefore keep a record of your recommendations and the reasoning that supports them in the form of letters written to the client.

A lady called about a small but troublesome tax situation. After a brief discussion, I said I did not think it practical to hire a tax lawyer, based on the amount in issue. She said, "I have no intention of hiring a lawyer. I just want the answers to my questions."

—A specialist in estate planning

Keep Up with the Client

We are not always thrilled to hear from insurance companies or stockbrokers who want to review our coverage or investments for us since it isn't always apparent that it is our interests that are uppermost in their minds. Lawyers reminding their clients about the need to review their wills may encounter the same skepticism. On the other hand, clients aren't happy to be forgotten either.

Style in Wills and Trusts

The writers of wills and trusts often have to lay aside the ideal of good writing, sometimes because of the ponderous and overwrought quality of legal writing in the field, particularly in the tax area, and sometimes because clients aren't as satisfied by simple, straightforward writing in such documents. But the turgid and indecipherable writing we find in wills and trust documents cannot always be justified as contributing to client satisfaction. Consider the following sentence from an actual trust document:

> *THIRD. If under the provisions of subparagraph (b) of subparagraph (2) of subparagraph C or*

paragraph FIRST of this indenture or under the provisions of subparagraph (6) of subparagraph D of paragraph SECOND of this indenture any property would become distributable to any beneficiary who is then under the age of twenty-one (21) years then instead of so distributing said property to such beneficiary the trustees may, in their sole and absolute discretion, distribute said property in trust, as a separate trust fund, to the trustees of the trust from which such distribution is to be made acting hereunder as trustees of such trust at the time of the termination of such trust, as trustees of said trust fund, and to their successors in trust.

Compare:

If any beneficiary under 21 years old becomes eligible for a distribution under the following provisions [specify below], the trustees may at their discretion distribute the property as a separate trust fund to the trustees of the fund from which the distribution is made. . . [We confess we cannot decipher the intention of the last two lines of the original].

Undoubtedly the worst abusers of the English language are those lawyers who have spent much time in the drafting of wills and trusts. If anything has worked once, be sure that the scrivener (an appropriate word for one who writes wills and trusts) will use it again. And again. And in many cases would be well-advised to do so.

The longest paragraphs in legal writing may be found in the Internal Revenue Code. One is 522 words long. The

A man finally went to see a lawyer to make his will. As they talked, the lawyer asked some questions about the estate of the prospective client's wife that he couldn't answer. That night when the man asked his wife about these matters, she told him that the same lawyer had done her will a few years earlier.
Not reassuring.

—A senior partner

Compare:

7. I leave the rest of my estate to the Home For Sick Cats.

with

ARTICLE SEVENTH: I give, devise and bequeath all the rest, residue, and remainder of my estate, real, personal or mixed, to the Institute for the Care and Sustenance of Members of the Species Felix Domesticus.

One can almost hear the tones of Big Ben in the distance. In this area, client satisfaction suffered a serious setback when wax seals and ribbons on documents went out of style.

—A senior partner

provision in the Code that deals with the marital deduction from Federal Estate Tax is a 200-word paragraph. It is so obscure that estate planners don't dare paraphrase it and merely insert it word for word in a will or trust. One estate planner observed that he spends about 25% of his time trying to explain to clients what that paragraph is intended to do (it is impossible to explain what it says).

There is no room for originality in writing wills and trusts. It is best to find the language in another document, preferably one that has survived tax litigation.

6 Rewrite for Effectiveness

To be effective writers, lawyers must above all be willing to *rewrite*. Rewriting is crucial to effective writing. All the effective writers we know make time to do it. Still, many lawyers don't rewrite, or don't rewrite enough. Some feel they don't have time. Some feel they don't know how to rewrite so as to make a significant difference. This chapter shows how to make time for rewriting and how to get better at it. Along the way, it highlights principles of revision from earlier chapters and extends the discussion of effective writing into matters of legal style.

> Nothing you write, if you hope to be any good, will ever come out as you first hoped.
>
> —Lillian Hellman

To begin with, legal writers must not imagine the purview of revision and rewriting too narrowly. "Revision" is sometimes talked about as if it is a matter only of "cleaning up," or "polishing," or "correcting" a draft through "proofreading," or perhaps "editing" for "style." This view blinds writers to some of the most important ways their writing can be rewritten to be made more effective.

Rewriting involves all of the following:

- the largest kind of *rethinking* of the whole project

  What *is* the issue in this case anyway? What is it I want this letter to *do*? What's the purpose of this contract?

- *selecting and arranging the materials to be presented*

  How do I tell the story of the facts in this matter? Which of my arguments will be most effective with this reader? Do I want it first or last?

- *editing for style and syntax*

  How do I arrange clauses, phrases, and words in sentences and sentences in paragraphs?

- *editing for diction*

  How do I choose the most effective words?

- *proofreading*

  How do I produce writing that is correct according to the conventions of citation, punctuation, and spelling?

Most writers rewrite throughout the writing process. It is helpful, however, to separate the writing process into stages. Early writing is often more productive when we don't worry too much about matters better dealt with when we edit or correct a draft. Proofreading should be postponed until we're pretty well satisfied that larger changes are no longer called for. Why correct what will later be cut?

The most effective order for the stages of the rewriting process may or may not be the one that appears in the list above. The important thing to remember is that it is usually helpful to concentrate on one kind of rewriting at a time, but that writing and rewriting can loop back on itself: changes of one kind can lead to changes of another. This looping back is quite likely, for example, when you rearrange your paragraphs or sentences. To the alert rewriter, the new arrangement almost always suggests other helpful changes. Even when you change your diction—deciding, for example, to write "Ms. Johnson applied" rather than "An application was made"— you may then be able to see other kinds of changes that would make your writing more effective.

To begin with, writers and rewriters need to ask whether they are writing to develop their thinking or rewriting for a reader. The two kinds of writing tend to have very different features.

Writing as Thinking (Discovery)	Writing for Readers (Communication)
Propositions	
Point at end	Point at top
Sentence Structure	
Topics at end	Topics at top
Verbs separated from subjects	Verbs close to subjects
Logical structure	
Episodic:	Analytic:
X and Y and Z and A	If X and Y and Z, then A and B

Writers who are thinking tend naturally to produce text that has the features on the left. Writers who have had to give a lot of thought to what they want to say must usually make conscious efforts to rewrite for readers so that their drafts have the features listed on the right. If we know we have been thinking hard about a problem, as lawyers often do, we can expect to need to revise language that looks like thinking into language that works for a reader.

When writers turn to rewriting with the reader in mind, they can easily be led to rethink their whole undertaking. Rewriters frequently find themselves crossing back-and-forth between rewriting for readers and rethinking. Still it is helpful to distinguish the two kinds of rewriting. Lawyers take an important step toward learning how to rewrite for readers simply by realizing that much of the demanding writing they do will be writing-as-thinking to begin with, not writing-for-the-reader.

Rewriting for the reader is work, but it need not be only a chore. When lawyers see their rewriting making a difference, what is true for professional writers can become true for them as legal writers: rewriting can become the most rewarding part of writing.

The pleasure *is* the rewriting: The first sentence can't be written until the final sentence is written. This is a koan-like statement, and I don't mean to sound needlessly obscure or mysterious, but it's simply true. The completion of any work automatically necessitates its revisioning.
—Joyce Carol Oates

First drafts are for learning what your novel or story is about. Revision is working with that knowledge to enlarge and enhance an idea, to re-form it . . . . Revision is one of the true pleasures of writing.
—Bernard Malamud

If any man wishes to write a clear style, let him first be clear in his thoughts.
—Johann W. von Goethe

Rewrite to Develop Thinking

To write effectively, writers must be clear about their purposes. But how is this clarity of purpose best achieved? Should we expect it to be achieved *before* writing, as the quotation from Goethe suggests? Not very often, if at all, especially in the challenging situations legal writers must deal with. For lawyers, writing and rewriting are especially powerful tools for achieving clarity of purpose and understanding.

We start thinking precisely because something *isn't* clear, because the solution to a problem isn't obvious or automatic. Actual thinking can't be observed directly, but we can infer what it looks like to some extent from transcripts of oral conversations, which can be appalling in their incoherence. Here is a supposed transcript of an oral judgment, given to us by a Canadian judge:

> *Ah – yes – I follow that – but I am not sure where it takes us – I, er – [inaudible] the point could be, that, but [unintelligible] but it could be otherwise. It could be so in some other case because the key here is the issue of well, identity, I don't really mean identity, I mean reliability, I mean credibility. I mean, you know, has the Crown done it or not? The golden thread sort of stuff – I thought that after Mr. Grey was finished they hadn't done it – but they have. Everything is here – rather there, and I don't have much – I mean any hesitation in concluding – notwithstanding the able points made by Mr. White – I mean Grey – so eloquently that you are, after all is said and done, with everything considered, you are guilty.*

Think before you speak is criticism's motto; speak before you think is creation's.

—E. M. Forster

This "transcript" clearly represents thinking though not what we would call clear thinking. For all sorts of reasons, it isn't effective writing for a judgment. The defendant is guilty, for now, no matter how the reasons are written, but the hesitations reflected in the transcript wouldn't do the judge any good if the judgment were to be appealed.

If, however, this were a transcript not of a judgment but instead the judge's reflections to himself about the case, the writing would be effective. It apparently does lead the judge to a clear understanding of how to decide the case. The judge is now in a much better position to deliver an effective judgment, perhaps something like:

> *I believe the witnesses who testified that the officers of the Crown did what they were supposed to do. I find the defendant guilty.*

If the judge is to be able to rewrite the "draft" as it needs to be rewritten, he or she needs to take the original transcript as notes of *thinking*, rather than as a *draft* of the final judgment. Some who counsel legal writers to think *before* writing fear that we will get too invested in what we have written to rewrite it as we should, especially when it comes to cutting irrelevant material. We tend to get more invested in something we take to be a draft than in something we take as notes, or plans, or thoughts. This investment in what we have already written may impede the rewriting that would make our work more effective.

If writing is to be effective as *thinking*, we must not become too invested in it as a *draft*. Thinking and planning *are* crucial for effective writers. Effective drafting arises out of effective planning. But thinking and planning usually go forward best through writing that is done for that purpose.

General Strategies for Rewriting before, during, and after Writing

In this section,
Talk
Ask Questions
Freewrite
Make an Image
Read Aloud
Outline before Writing a Draft
Outline after Writing a Draft

Revision and rewriting are about learning to see in new ways. To do it effectively, we have to loosen the hold our current thinking, or our current draft, has on us so that we may see how to make it more effective. The following familiar activities can help anyone who is committed to writing more effectively. Some will be more useful for certain kinds of revision than others, as we will point out below. To realize how helpful they can be for rewriting, lawyers need actually to try them out for that purpose. We provide exercises.

Talk. Lawyers frequently use talk to think and to test their ideas. For talk to help with rewriting, however, it needs to be accompanied by a certain kind of listening—listening for sentences as well as for ideas—and it needs to be done with pencil in hand—so that the more effective ideas and sentences can be written down.

Lawyers talk to other lawyers most of the time. But professionals talking to other professionals can fall into conventional modes of thought and language from which they may need to be rescued by efforts to explain matters to someone who doesn't know much, or anything, about the law or the matter at hand. Talking to non-lawyers also helps with tone and diction (see pp. 146-158) as lawyers try to find plain language to say what they mean.

> *Exercise*: With pencil and pad in hand, take 5 minutes or so to explain to your secretary some complex matter you are working on. Listen to what you say and make notes. Or ask your secretary to make notes about what he or she hears you say. See if your answer provides language that would be more effective in your draft.

Ask Questions. Lawyers ask each other questions that help them rethink matters. Lawyers can also ask themselves helpful questions about what they have written. Many helpful questions are implicit in the principles set out in this book. Among the more important

- What do I want this letter to DO?

- What am I really saying here?

- Who will read this? What do they need to know if this writing is to do what I want it to do?

- What is my strongest argument?

- What do the makers of this agreement want to accomplish through the agreement?

Ask these questions *outside* of the terms of any draft you may have written. Try to get a distance from your current thinking and language. A good question to ask yourself when you have gotten bogged down in the details of an argument is "What am I REALLY trying to say here?" Use your response to the question as a new starting point.

> *Exercise*: Ask one of the questions above of something you have written, and write out your answer in ordinary language, if possible, without referring to anything you have written in the draft. See if your answer provides language that would be more effective in your draft.

Freewrite. Freewriting can help you focus, expand, and reformulate your thoughts. Freewriting is also called automatic writing. It amounts to writing out fast and continuously whatever comes to mind during a specified amount of time. It is a technique for thinking, not for drafting, though it can produce some "keepers." A good time to freewrite is when you've gotten stuck. It's also a good way to get started if you are paralyzed by a blank page or screen.

Five or ten minutes of freewriting will produce a lot of stuff that isn't helpful and that you will discard. You write, however, expecting that the sentences will carry you in some fashion toward your goal, and they almost always do. A productive way of freewriting is to write for five minutes, stop, read what you have written, pick one sentence that seems promising, and beginning with that sentence, write for another five minutes . Writers who spend twenty minutes doing this will often find that they have much more good material than does the writer who spends twenty minutes trying to write the perfect draft.

> *Exercise*: Keeping loosely in mind some challenging matter you are working on (a tricky letter, a complex contract, a motion), write for five minutes, read what you have written, circle one sentence, write for another five minutes beginning with that sentence, do this one more time. Do not be concerned if you "stray" during the five minutes of continuous writing. See if at the end of this 15+ minutes you have produced language that would be effective in a draft.

Make an Image. This activity helps you focus on the overall shape of your writing and the relation of its elements. An outline is an image of writing, but many other images are possible. Two others are the chain that we used above to represent writing as thinking and the inverted tree structure we used to represent writing for a reader. A particular writing might be represented as a spiral, or a series of connected nodes, or a Venn diagram, or rings in a pond. We sometimes produce these images as we doodle.

The mental exercise of stepping back from something you have written to represent it as an image can help you see how it might be rewritten to be more effective. Trial lawyers are urged to make maximum use of visuals in courtroom presentations. Writers can use visuals to help them rewrite.

> *Exercise*: Playfully, and without worrying about artistic merit, make a pictorial image of something you have written as it now is. Now draw another image of the way the writing might be rewritten. Consider which version would be more effective.

Read Aloud. Reading drafts aloud is an infallible way of identifying opportunities for rewriting. It is instructive whether one reads to a live listener or aloud to oneself, though reading to a listener is usually more provocative, whether the listener responds or not. Uttering one's language somehow activates all sorts of critical resources. For this activity to work, however, the reader must listen to what the voice is doing, and make notes in the text. If your voice goes dead as you are reading, or if you find yourself saying "blah-blah-blah," you can be sure that you are learning how this language will be experienced by your reader, and that you have located language that needs to be rewritten. If you stumble, the language made you stumble, and will make your reader stumble, and must be rewritten. If you feel effort, your reader will too. If you think something needs to be added, your reader will too.

It is usually best to read through the whole document before returning to the places that need to be rewritten. As you read, you can make notes like "?" or "+" or "!" or "oof"

No style is good that is not fit to be spoken or read aloud with effect.

— William Hazlitt

or "blah" to designate places to which your voice is saying you should return.

> *Exercise*: With pencil in hand, read aloud a page or more of something you have written, preferably with a listener present. Read continuously and make quick notes in the margin where your voice tells you something is not as it should be. Rewrite to address the problems. Reread the pages aloud. New problems may present themselves. Don't be discouraged. You are learning to write more effectively.

Outline before Writing a Draft. We can use general outlines sometimes to get started. But we should not confuse such outlines with those that help us give the most effective shape to the final product.

A common general outline of a brief or judicial opinion, for example, is

- Facts

- Law

- Conclusion

Before a lawyer or a judge writes a brief or opinion, it will be necessary to marshal the facts. But the outline here is inadequate for the final version of the writing. Lawyers reading reported opinions know that too many of them begin by presenting facts before the reader has been given any way of understanding what they have to do with the issue and the decision.

A better general outline for a draft of an opinion would be

- Issue

- Facts

- Law

- Judgment

or better yet

- Specific issue with facts necessary to understand it

- Discussion of each part of issue with facts pertinent to that part, in an order predictable from statement of the issue,

- Judgment

A lawyer reading a judge's statement of the "specific issue with facts necessary to understand it" is given real guidance about the shape of the written decision. When judges begin to write, however, they may not know exactly how they want to formulate the issue. A general understanding of the issue hovers in the background as judges begin thinking about the facts of the case. The opinion that has been rewritten for the reader will begin with a specific formulation of the issue.

It may take a while to arrive at the specific formulation that is needed. A statement like "The issue in this case is negligence" provides a place for the writer to get started, but it provides scant guidance to writer or reader about what will follow. Better would be a statement like "The issue in this case is whether the county failed to maintain the roadway in proper condition, and whether that failure led to the accident." The outline implicit here is

1. Was the roadway not in proper condition?

2. Did this condition come about because the county failed to maintain the road?

3. Did the condition cause the accident?

What if you have arrived at a statement of the issue but in your discussion find yourself writing in ways that don't follow the lines set out by the statement? Instead of chiding yourself for your lack of discipline, consider whether your writing has led you to a point where you can now see how to rewrite the statement of the issue to make it more effective. Writing often leads writers to think in productive ways that following the outline too closely would preclude.

Outline after Writing a Draft. After we have produced a draft, it may be helpful to produce an outline of the draft as it has actually emerged. If we find that we can outline the material easily and that the outline has direction and balance, we can feel confident about how we have shaped our material. If we cannot outline the material easily, the outline may help us see what we must do to organize and develop the material more effectively.

To be useful, these outlines of your drafts must be written in *sentences*, not just topic headings. Consider how much *less* useful the outline above would be in the form

1. Condition

2. Maintenance

3. Cause

This outline gives the writer no useful information about what the sections are dealing with or how they are related to each other. The advice we are giving here follows advice given elsewhere about stating issues effectively in briefs (pp. 63-64).

A headnote writer (somebody does write those, you know) said you could easily tell how well-written an opinion was by how easy it was to write the headnotes.

Rewrite Drafts for Readers

Read Drafts Critically

To rewrite for readers we must learn to *read our drafts critically* and see them as our intended readers are likely to see them. Activities of the kind suggested above can help us do this. Finally, however, rewriting for a reader is an act of imagination, and of sympathy and respect. Lawyers know better than others that readers who have to struggle with what they are reading react not just with incomprehension but with animus, as if they have been insulted. In a way, they have been.

Learn to think of readers not as mere recipients of information but as people who are experiencing the language as they move through it, as if they were watching a play rather than being filled up with "content." Readers and play-watchers aren't just sitting there "taking it all in." They are (usually subconsciously) asking questions, getting their hopes up, raising objections, experiencing satisfaction or frustration, or wondering how things will turn out—assuming, of course, that they haven't fallen asleep or given up in frustration or disgust.

Style is effectiveness
of assertion.
—George Bernard Shaw

Style is the man him-
self.
—Georges de Buffon

Much of what we address in this chapter has to do with *style*. The word "style" can direct our attention to a wide range of issues. At one level, it can refer only to what are sometimes called the "mechanics" of writing, matters we address by "proofreading." At another it can refer to almost everything having to do with the act of writing.

Either usage is fine as long as equivocation doesn't mislead about the range of choices effective writers must make and lead us to conclude that a "correct" or "good" style is necessarily an effective one. Our concern here is with effective style.

Correctness—in such matters as spelling, punctuation, quoting and citing authority—is crucial to effective legal writing. It demonstrates a seriousness of purpose, a concern for accuracy, a respect for the opposition and the court. Carelessness in such matters reflects a lack of respect for the reader, which is repaid in kind.

An effective style is more than a correct style and more, even, than a clear style. An effective style helps to develop the purpose of the writer and to motivate the reader. To achieve an effective style, writers have to do more than learn the principles of good writing, important as they may be. We have to learn how style contributes to effectiveness in different situations and how to choose wisely from our stylistic options.

In what follows we offer advice that will help you *edit for style and syntax, edit for effective diction, edit for effective citation and quotation,* and *proofread for spelling and effective punctuation.* Our treatment of the issues that can arise here is not exhaustive. We deal with what seems to us to contribute most to effective legal writing. At the end of the book we provide a bibliography for lawyers who might want to pursue particular matters further.

A Rough but Serviceable Glossary of Grammatical Terms

1. Phrase

A group of words that acts as a unit but falls short of a clause (like "a group of words," or "of a clause.")

2. Clause

A group of words that acts as a unit and that has a subject and a predicate. All sentences are clauses but some clauses aren't sentences, such as "which are included" (a relative clause) or "although she achieved a breakthrough" (a dependant clause).

3. Preposition

Words like *of, by, through, in, about*, that connect another word to a noun, as in *cause* (noun) of (preposition) *action* (word connected to "cause")."

4. Syntax

Word order, sentence structure

5. Diction

Word choice, vocabulary

6. Relative Pronoun

A word that stands for an antecedent noun, such as *it, this, that*, and *which*. Writers often fail to make clear what the antecedent is.

7. Nominalization

A word formed when a verb or adjective is rendered as a noun, such as when *apply* becomes *application*, *procure* becomes *procurement*, and *name* becomes *nominalization*.

8. Parallelism

When grammatical form follows function, as in "I came, I saw, I conquered," as opposed to "I came, I saw it, it was conquered by me."

9. Passive voice

When the object of an action is made the grammatical subject of a sentence, as in "It was conquered." Notice that this grammatical form allows the writer to avoid saying who did it.

10. Active Voice

When the doer of an action is also the subject of the sentence, as in "I wrote it and I like it like that."

Effective lawyers respect their tools, which are found not in law alone, but in the language. Lawyers who use language carelessly inspire as much confidence as carpenters who leave their saws out in the rain.

Judge Chambers's opinions rarely exceeded two pages. And he was rarely reversed. A commentator once accused him of being "cryptic." All in all, it was probably better that he was able to meet the requirements of the United States Supreme Court, which he was able to do even though that court is not renowned for the brevity and concision of its opinions.

Rewrite for Brevity and Conciseness

Brevity requires not using unnecessary words. Only when we have a clear and precise understanding of our purpose and reader, however, can we decide what is unnecessary. In the complex matters lawyers deal with, precise understandings of purpose and audience may be arrived at only after considerable thought and writing. Brevity, it follows, will be accomplished only through revision.

"Brief" means short. "Concise" means short *and* sharp. Effective writing will always be sharp in its thinking but, as we have seen, it won't always be brief or even clear to all readers. Certain clients will not appreciate brevity in documents prepared for them. Some judges seem to weigh arguments by the pound. Lawyers are sometimes wise not to improve bad writing that has value as precedent or has been approved by the IRS.

Highly respected lawyers are more likely to be given the benefit of the doubt by clients and judges in these matters, but even the great Elihu Root had to defend himself to his client for writing a one-page will (see pp. 115-121). One's peers will usually appreciate conciseness. But it *is* possible to overdo succinctness. If the brief presentation or reply is construed as curt, it may not be effective.

Lawyers will sometimes explain their unnecessarily long and wordy writing on the grounds that they don't have time to be brief. These will be the same lawyers who say they don't have time to revise. They may be speaking truth. They probably put off writing for so long that they ran out of time. Nor do they know how to revise efficiently. This can explain a failure to revise. It does not justify it.

Shortening a document is time-consuming when you are trying to shorten a document that wanders all over the place and is uncertain in its focus. Cutting out unnecessary words is only part of what such a draft needs. Once you have developed a clear sense of purpose and a good plan for your draft through early writing, it will take far less time to shorten your document. If you decide to work at being brief, you will get better at it over time.

Lawyers do have to spend a lot of time wading through other people's unclear and over-long prose. The public may think that is what lawyers are for. They may even think that lawyers are supposed to write such stuff. Lawyers themselves ought to know better.

If you decide that a particular situation calls for a long document, remember that the thinking reflected in the longer document must still be sharp and focused. Judges and clients who think long documents reflect a greater seriousness of purpose will be persuaded by them only if the parts they do read are clear and effective. They will read the parts

> At Gettysburg, Edward Everett spoke first, followed by President Lincoln. The next day, Mr. Everett wrote to Lincoln, "I should be glad if I can flatter myself that I came as near the central idea of the occasion in two hours as you did in two minutes." Mr. Everett, Lincoln's peer, saw how good the speech was. It has been reported, however, that many in the crowd that day found Lincoln's little speech disappointing.

Checklist: Brevity and Conciseness

- Concise thinking is necessary to effective writing whether the document is brief or long.

- We can often arrive at concise thinking more quickly by letting early writing take us there.

- Brevity and concise thinking are accomplished only through rewriting.

- To achieve brevity, write early, expecting to revise and select out what is necessary to your purpose and reader.

- Be brief when brevity would be effective.

- Brevity is usually preferred for one's peers.

- Decide what isn't necessary by referring to your purpose and intended reader

- To achieve brevity, write early, expecting to revise and select only what is necessary to your purpose and reader.

that summarize the arguments and conclusions. These should be carefully rewritten. Computers have given us the capacity to import great hunks of text into our documents to make them longer, if need be. But if an argument is to be persuasive, a brief's statements of the issues and its summaries of the facts and law must still be as concise and accessible as possible.

The lawyers who have the best chance of achieving brevity and concision in a document are the ones who begin a writing task early—planning and writing freely because they know they will be cutting much of what they produce at first.

Jeremy Bentham called judge-made common law "dog law," because it taught its lessons the way many people teach their dogs, by punishing them for what they have done after they have done it. My psychology professor told the story of a dog he had who loved to chase cars, noisily and enthusiastically. The professor hated to have his dog chase cars in that quiet neighborhood, so, when the dog returned, tail wagging, tongue lolling and full of elation, the professor would run out, grab the dog, admonish it, and throw it into his basement. It was not a bright dog, and it took several months for it to get the idea. It would then chase the cars with roars of defiance, come trotting happily back and jump into the basement on his own.

—A trial lawyer

E.B. White wrote that Professor Strunk's refrain was "Omit needless words, omit needless words, omit needless words." Doesn't this violate his own precept? Here the repetition is an attempt to communicate the almost despairing urgency of his feeling on this point. It is more effective *because* it violates the precept.

At the level of the sentence, "wordiness" is the opposite of concision, and it is pandemic in legal language. We address this problem in the section on Diction.

Rewrite for Effective Repetition and Redundancy

Repetition is one of the enemies of brevity. Repetition and redundancy decrease effectiveness when they seem to be *only* repeating something—that is, when they do nothing to advance the argument or assist the reader. But engineers build redundancy into systems so that if one aspect of the system fails, another will back it up. This kind of redundancy can make legal writing more effective. It helps to repeat one's key points in the places where they have the best chance of being noticed by busy readers. Lawyers will have to exercise judgment about what will seem excessive here.

The *structure* of your writing should be predictable. If you write a sentence "The structure of your writing should be predictable," your next sentence should follow in a way that advances the discussion of the topic, perhaps by offering an example. Normally, a sentence should not simply repeat the sentence that precedes it: it should add new information of some kind, repeating the theme of the preceding sentence. Repetition of this kind helps the reader stay on track.

We may have heard that it is a good thing to vary our language to keep from boring a reader. But in legal writing, we may confuse the reader by varying key terms. If we use the word "negligence" in one paragraph and "fault" in the next, the reader will wonder if we are talking about the same thing or something different. Do not vary key terms.

For effective repetition

- Match the structure of your argument to the expectations created by your introductions of the whole piece.

- Repeat key points in key places.

- Do not vary key terms.

To avoid ineffective repetition

- Condense references.

- Make sure that your repetition assists the reader.

Rewrite for Effective Sentences

In this section,
    Find and Rewrite Unreadable Sentences
    Rewrite for Effective Verbs and Nouns
       Reduce Nominalization
       Increase Active Voice
       Use Real Verbs: "To Be" or Not "To Be"
    Rewrite for Emphasis
    Rewrite for Effective Transitions

Find and Rewrite Unreadable Sentences. People think it is length that makes sentences hard to read. But what makes sentences hard to read is

- they do not let the reader know early what the main clause is, either because the writer buries it or because the writer interposes too many words between the subject and the predicate.

At the beginning of a hearing, the lawyer says, "The plaintiff, who has been pursuing this matter in the courts for four years, and we aren't even counting the time spent before suit was filed, nor are we mentioning here the expense to his spirit, let alone his pocketbook, since at this time it would not be appropriate to do so, is ready, your honor." Withholding the predicate is here a way of holding the floor.

or

- the writer does not connect a sentence to the sentence that precedes it or does not let the reader know early in the sentence how it follows from the point of the preceding sentence.

Opening of an opinion: "This issue in this case is negligence. The case is before us on appeal from the district court. Defendant has filed a cross-motion. . ." A great many opinions start out like this, unfortunately, except that the sentences are longer.

Shorter sentences usually are easier to read. But text that consists only of short sentences can seem choppy, brusque, immature, too informal. Legal writing is replete with long sentences that are hard to read. But long sentences that are well constructed are not necessarily harder to read than is a collection of short sentences that covers the same territory. A long sentence is badly constructed, from a reader's point of view, when the reader has to wade through a tangle of phrases and clauses without knowing what the foundation of the sentence is. Readers discover this foundation when they learn what the main clause is.

Are short paragraphs, then, more readable than long ones? The considerations that apply to sentences apply to paragraphs: shorter ones are usually easier to read (and thus are favored in newspaper journalism), but longer ones are not necessarily harder. Too many short paragraphs can seem journalistic or breezy, too many long ones lazy or pedantic. Any reader contemplating a page that presents no paragraph breaks in it experiences a definite sinking feeling.

Short paragraphs after long ones emphasize a point.

Lawyers and judges write sentences and paragraphs that are unreadable because they already know what the main clause or point is and are instead intent on the qualifications and modifications that must be included.

All of us write this way when we are thinking primarily about the problem we are dealing with. Writing of this kind is not bad writing when it occurs in a discovery draft. But before we present such writing to a reader, we must rewrite it, thinking primarily about how that reader will encounter the sentences.

Effective readable sentences are built by recognizing that a sentence has created particular questions or needs in the reader that the next sentence must address. Readable sentences address those questions or needs. For the reader, *sentences are events.* Writers should not think of them as containers that readers will be content to unpack until they locate the gizmo hidden somewhere amongst the wads of packing. Writers of readable sentences recognize that every sentence extends a hand that must be grasped in a timely way by the sentence that follows it.

Sentences aren't effective just because they are easy to read. Sentences are effective because they contribute to the purposes of the whole document. They are integrated with the sentences around them and through them integrated with the whole discourse. How is this integration achieved?

Each composition will integrate its meanings differently. For the lawyer, it is important to realize that effective sentences do more than knit up the pieces of the discourse or add information; they add energy. They take the torch offered by the previous sentence and carry it to the next sentence. They do more than just pass the torch: they add energy and increase the brightness of its flame.

Reading aloud is a good way of locating unreadable sentences. If you stumble, or strain, or get breathless while reading a sentence, it needs attention. Long sentences are always worth looking at. Finally, you can also begin to cultivate the habit of looking for the main clause of every sentence.

It is usually easy enough to improve sentences that are hard to read because they have been written by a writer who was thinking hard. First find the subject and the verb that constitute the main clause. They may appear together at the end of the sentence or be separated from each other by a number of qualifying words and phrases.

When you find the main clause, rewrite the sentence with main clause at or near the beginning and let the rest of the sentence develop out of it. Now you are in a better position to consider whether your sentence is effectively constructed in the context in which it appears. It may be that you will want to rewrite the sentence again to link it more clearly with the sentence that precedes it or the one that follows it.

Rewrite for Effective Verbs and Nouns. In legal writing, it is often hard to tell who is doing what to whom. The actors and action at the foundation of the legal matter disappear beneath a deep deposit of verbiage. Certain stylistic practices are responsible for this "disappearing" of actors and action. Effective legal writers must be aware of these stylistic practices and how they work.

Reduce Nominalization. In law school, we learn what has been called "the official style." No one teaches it. We learn it by osmosis. One feature of this style is that it is heavily nominalized. After law school, we need to learn when this style is effective and when it isn't.

Every book that discusses legal writing will tell you that you should not use so many nominalizations. There is a place for them, as there is a place for everything that the language can do. If we are to use nominalizations effectively, we need to understand what they are and how they work.

Nominalizations are nouns that used to be verbs or adjectives. "Nominalization" is one. The verb buried in it is "to nominate" or "to name." You can nominalize a verb by adding to it *–tion* (application), or *–ment* (averment), or *–ity* (clarity). Every nominalization is holding a verb beneath the surface. Legal writing (and much other "offical" writing) looks and sounds the way it does in part because it is heavily nominalized.

Why do lawyers favor these words instead of the verbs they come from? They've seen lots of nominalizations in the legal writing they have read, for one thing. For another, the actions lawyers perform usually involve doing things with documents. This could give them an inclination to say that a group "submitted an application," rather than that they "applied."

Nominalization allows the writer to obscure who is doing what to whom. "An application was made . . ." doesn't tell us who applied or to whom. If we rewrite the sentence around the verb *applied*, we cannot escape telling the reader who did the applying.

If most legal writing is heavily nominalized, then writing that uses the original verbs instead of the derived nominalizations may not sound like what people, including lawyers, have come to think of as legal writing. It may be more lively, it may give a clearer sense of who did what to whom. It won't sound so . . . official.

Nominalizations and passive voice constructions (discussed below) consort with each other regularly. More than any other stylistic feature they are responsible for the leaden quality of much legal writing.

Compare:

Agreement was reached concerning the applicability of the decision.

with

The IRS agreed to apply [not to apply?] the decision.

In the rewritten version, we now know not only who agreed (though we may have quite a time finding out just who in the IRS did the agreeing), but what was agreed to.

Note: *Decision* is also a nominalization but if it appears at the end of the sentence as it does here, it doesn't weigh the sentence down the way the nominalizations in the first version of the sentence do. Nor does it in this case obscure who is doing what to whom.

Why not write all the time in a "verbal," non-lawyerly, style? Because sometimes it isn't effective. "Plain English" may not be as effective—in terms of legal effect or in terms of client satisfaction—as "legal" English. Having given the devil nominalization its due, we must say that it is hard to imagine a situation in which it would be effective legal writing to label an order as follows (actual case):

Order Striking Affirmation in Opposition to Allowance of Claims Seeking the Disallowance of Invalid Claims.

Increase Active Voice. Caesar said, "Veni, vidi, vici," which we translate as "I came, I saw, I conquered." He spoke in the active voice, and we know who deserves the credit or blame for his actions. If he had wanted to dodge responsibility, or share it, he might have said "Visus sum" ("It was seen") and "Victus sum" ("It was conquered"). To sound even more contemporary, he might have used the euphemism "pacified," instead of "conquered."

A sentence is written in the active voice when the doer of the action appears as the subject of the sentence. A sentence written in the passive voice puts another noun, typically a nominalization, in the subject position, which allows the writer not to say who did the action, as in *Suit was filed* or *Application was made.* The passive voice allows us to evade responsibility because it allows us to avoid saying who did it. "Mistakes were made" doesn't say who made them. The question for legal writers is whether they are using the passive voice on purpose, to leave open the question of responsibility or to be tactful, or using it evasively or mindlessly, just because it sounds more like legal writing.

You will find your style changed to a startling extent if you decide to rewrite to use the passive voice as little as possible and decide also to unearth the verbs hidden in the nominalizations that spring so naturally to mind in the practice of law. Your style will be cleaner, sharper, more vivid, more pointed. This may make you nervous at first. You may feel . . . exposed. But persevere. You'll get over your nervousness and may even find that you are thinking more clearly.

Use Real Verbs: "To Be" or Not "To Be." "To be" is not a real verb, if by "verb" we mean a word that denotes action. In legal writing, forms of the verb "to be"—what we like call "izzies" and "wuzzies"—appear frequently, often in the company of dummy subjects, as in

> *There is an important case . . .*

> *It was found that . . .*

and in the company also of nominalizations and passive voice constructions, as in

> *Application was made . . .*

> *Judgment was entered . . .*

> *Service was made . . .*

> *Delivery was accomplished . . .*

> *A finding was made . . .*

The judge wrote: "The assurances fell on the fair side of a fine line between legality and illegality." A tactful way of designating a scoundrel.

Rewriters who want to achieve a more informative, active style—one relatively free of nominalizations and passive voice constructions—could begin by circling all forms of the word "to be" in their drafts and rewriting the sentences in which they appear. As we have said, the real verb often lurks in the nominalization (*apply, judge, serve, deliver, find* in the example above).

Rewrite for Emphasis. The most emphatic part of the sentence—and of the paragraph, the section, the motion, the brief—is the beginning. Put what you want to emphasize for the reader there—at the beginning. If you want to create suspense——rarely does effective legal writing want to do this—you might want to put it at the end. Do not allow it to be hidden in the middle. You put in the middle what you must mention but what you want to de-emphasize, like the "bad facts" of a case on appeal.

When you write legal argument, you are always trying to advance your theory of the case. The elements of that theory should appear in emphatic places. We advise legal writers to lead into a quotation, for example, with the claim that the quotation is there to establish, not with information about the source of the citation. (See Rewrite for Effective Quotation and Citation, pp. 162-168).

Punctuation can contribute to emphasis, but the exclamation point (pp. 172-173) must be used sparingly and with care. Graphic elements that create a LOUD text—like capital letters—are rarely effective in legal writing, any more than is a shout in the courtroom.

Rewrite for Effective Transitions. Transitions are created by the underlying musculature of the prose, not by the application of transition words as Velcro strips. Words like *therefore, however, consequently, in addition*, and *furthermore* only signal transitions: they don't create them. *Therefore* signals a logical inference. If the sentence that follows is doing something else, like simply adding information, the transition word will not create the transition.

Readers don't always read from sentence to sentence. Sometimes they skip around, and transition words can give readers signals that will help them negotiate the journey from sentence to sentence and section to section. Some transition words are more informative than others. "Therefore" signals a change in the kind of thing the next sentence will be doing—it says it will be drawing a conclusion from what preceded it. *In addition* tells the reader only that something else of the same kind is coming. *First* promises that there will be a *Second* and maybe a *Third*. These can help a reader read efficiently, or confuse the reader, when a *First* doesn't deliver on its implied promise of a *Second*.

Every sentence creates expectations about what will happen in the next sentence. If the next sentence ignores those expectations, readers lose track. The first sentence in this paragraph, which asserts that sentences create expectations in readers, might cause a reader to ask "So what?" Or "What is an example of this?" Or, "How is this pertinent to the question of what makes sentences effective?" The second sentence in the paragraph offers an answer to the first of these questions. If the second sentence had ignored the questions it raised for the reader—by going on to assert, for example, "Lawyers have a lot in common with poets"—then the reader might well have begun to wonder where we were going with this.

At appropriate moments, a new twist, an abrupt departure from what has come to be expected, may add to the force of the presentation. Poets sometimes build in disruptions to invite readers into an enlarged sense of what the language is doing. Readers of these poets can feel frustrated until they develop this enlarged sense. Afterwards, they can see why the language was used as it was, why their expectations weren't met immediately. In most legal writing, the disruptions and difficulties readers experience aren't intended. But on the appropriate occasion, and for purposes different from those of this book, a second sentence that disrupted the reader's expectations might be effective, as long as the writer went on finally to fulfill the expectations and desires created by both sentences.

Effective Writing

Rewrite for Effective Organization

For readability, the organization of a text needs to be predictable. Writing is predictable when it keeps the promises that are made and fulfills the expectations created by effectively written opening statements, statements of the issues, and first paragraphs in letters.

The organization of writing-as-thinking does not allow a reader to predict what is coming next. Writers learn to begin writing wherever they can—with notes, lists, dictated thoughts, free-writing. The goal here is to begin, to get words written that will help us think and put us in a better position to rewrite our thoughts and words to make them effective for a reader.

Writers rarely begin writing what the *reader* needs first. Writers facing the blank page or screen need to get started solving their writerly problems. Readers facing the written text need to get oriented to what writers have finally decided they want to do. What readers need at the beginning is not what the writer begins with but the distilled results of the writing process.

In effective written legal argument, paragraphs are not linked horizontally as they are in a simple story—a [and then] b [and then] c [and then] d, but hierarchically—a, b, and c support P, which leads to the further conclusion that JJ ... and so on. The shape and detail of this structure is what the legal writer struggles to discover at the early stages of the case. In the end, effective legal writers will be able to organize the major and minor propositions of their final drafts according to such a structure.

Legal writers can check for predictability by creating sentence outlines *after* they have completed a draft (see p. 131). A good exercise is to make a list of the first sentences of every paragraph and see if they suggest a predictable movement.

When legal writers rely on familiar (to them) patterns, they can fail to give the reader what is needed. It doesn't help to read at the beginning of a letter "We are in receipt of yours of 2 April ..." or to read at the beginning of an opinion a long account of the "Facts" before being told what the issue is.

Headings can help readers find their way through a text. Some headings don't help much. The more helpful headings are those that set out a topic fully in a sentence or clause. Like the argumentative headings in a brief, they inform the reader more specifically about what is to follow. "Issues" is unhelpful as a heading, compared to "Did Mr. Jones' Letter of January 1 Modify the Terms of the Contract?" This heading conveys specific information to the reader about what is to follow. "Issues" could be followed by almost anything.

In rewriting for effective organization, lawyers must ask questions about *import*, not just about predictability: What is my most important argument? What is the best way to tell the factual story? In such matters, lawyers have to rely on experience and the intuition developed from it more than any formula.

Rewrite for Effective Diction

In this section,

> Brief History of Legal Diction in English
> Rewrite for Effective Tone
>> How to Avoid Pretentious Language
>> How to Avoid Ineffective Legalese
>> Numerals
>> How to Avoid Ineffective Jargon
>> How to Avoid Sexist Language
> Rewrite to Avoid Wordiness
> Effective and Ineffective Platitudes
> Effective and Ineffective Boilerplate
> Find the Exact Word

The diction of legal writing is an easy mark, and it is often criticized, especially by advocates of "plain English." When the goal is effective legal writing, "plain English" may not always fill the bill. Nevertheless, lawyers who wish to be effective legal writers must pay close attention to their diction and make wise choices. Knowing the history of legal language can help.

Brief History of Legal Diction in English. The language of the law carries evidence of its complex history. All languages are polyglot, and English is more polyglot than most. Until the sixteenth century, what we now call "England" was not a single nation, as we now understand the term. Until 1066, the "English" that was spoken in the British Isles was a collection of Germanic dialects often as different from each other as Modern German is from Modern Dutch, or Modern Danish from Modern Norwegian. In 1066, when the Norman French defeated the English at the Battle of Hastings, the situation became at the same time simpler and more complicated. It became simpler because Norman French was imposed as the exclusive language of the English courts. It became more complicated because Norman French was thus added to what was already spoken in England.

French, a Romance language, is derived from Latin. At the time of the Norman conquest, Latin itself—though technically a dead language—was the language of the Church. When the first universities were founded, in the twelfth century, Latin was their official language, whether they were in Oxford, Paris, or Bologna.

Modern English, which developed out of the medieval London dialect—the dialect of Chaucer—began to dominate vernacular usage in the fourteenth century. In 1362, the Statute of Pleading was adopted, abolishing pleading in French. It commenced "Pleadings shall be pleaded in the English tongue." That is, it commenced with the French words which we may translate so. Ironically, the Statute of Pleading had to be written entirely in French. Pleadings were entirely oral then. If a writ or order became necessary, it was usually in Latin.

By 1650, England had evolved into something like its modern form as a nation-state, and Parliament passed a law requiring English to be used in all processes and proceedings. But English was still the tongue of the "vulgar" (that is, etymologically, "of the people"). French was everywhere in the courts. Latin was still the language of higher learning; law books were published in Latin or French, not the vulgar tongue "lest the unlearned might read but not understand." Paper pleadings were coming into use at this time as well.

In this world, lawyers had to choose between

the French	and the English:
devise	*bequeath*
gibbet	*gallows*
infant	*child*
larceny	*theft*
marriage	*wedding*
property	*goods*
pledge	*borrow*

They did not dare choose one or the other, so they used both. The common law being what it is, many of these usages have persisted. As a result we now have bilingual synonyms galore:

> *devise and bequeath*
> *deem and consider*
> *final and conclusive*
> *fit and proper*
> *free and clear*
> *give, devise, and bequeath*
> *goods and chattels*
> *had and received*
> *keep and maintain*
> *in lieu, in place, instead*
> *maintenance and upkeep*
> *made and provided*
> *mind and memory*
> *new and novel*
> *pardon and forgive*
> *peace and quiet*
> *save and except*
> *right, title, and interest*
> *shun and avoid*
> *will and testament*
> *give, devise and bequeath*
> *rest, residue, remainder*
> *remise, release and quit-claim*
> *grant, bargain, sell, convey*

As recently as at the adoption of the Uniform Probate Code, *devise*, the word from the French, has displaced *bequeath*, from the vulgar English tongue.

—A trusts and estates lawyer

Effective Writing

From time to time, critics of English have complained about the contamination of "pure" English by "foreign" words. These critics will certainly be among those who want "[f]irst of all [to] kill all the lawyers." Nor will they have much patience with writers like Jorge Luis Borges, the Argentinean and recipient of the Nobel Prize for literature, who said he preferred to write in English because of its unparalleled expressive resources, which stemmed not from its purity but from its richness and complexity. In any case, the history of legal language provides a helpful backdrop for considering what makes legal diction effective.

Rewrite for Effective Tone. Effective writers are always alert to the *tone* of their writing. Tone communicates a writer's attitude toward the reader and the subject and can have an enormous effect on effectiveness.

Lawyers are not trained to be alert to the tone of their writing. In college and law school, we probably have used only the relatively formal tone of academic writing. In court papers, the tone is almost always formal, although carefully chosen moments of informality can add emphasis. The tone of letters can vary widely, however. Effective legal writers do not use the same tone in writing to a grieving spouse that they use in demand letters.

Reading our writing to live audiences who are under no particular obligation to be respectful helps us to identify inappropriate tone. Listeners who don't have to pretend they know what we are talking about can help us find places where we lose our audiences, if we do not allow ourselves to dismiss their difficulties as the product of their lay status. Office staff are an overlooked resource here. If we can't find willing listeners, we can learn much by reading our drafts aloud to ourselves. To get the benefit of this exercise, we must listen to the words and sentences, not just mouth them.

The issue can be complicated by an audience's expectations. Lincoln's address at Gettysburg on the Fourth of July consisted of ten sentences and 266 words, 191 of which were one-syllable. It was short, simple, and unpretentious, and many in the crowd were disappointed by it. Like some

Not all "doublets" combine the Latinate with the Germanic. Consider *food and water*, an English doublet, and its Latinate equivalent *nutrition and hydration*. Which is the better expression for a Living Will that will be read by clients contemplating their death, and possibly by doctors?

—A trusts and estates lawyer

A past chairman of the Civil Aeronautics Board, Alfred E. Kahn, in making a plea to his staff for "straightforward, quasi-conversational, humane prose," told a young lawyer who wanted to say "we deem it appropriate" to ask himself how that would go over with his children.

people having their wills drawn, they wanted it to be impressive. The two-hour speech Everett made on the occasion was more like it, they thought. No one reads Everett's speech today, but that doesn't mean it was ineffective under the circumstances. We may like to think that if we had been in the audience that day we would have found Lincoln's speech more effective. Perhaps we would have, perhaps not.

How to Avoid Pretentious Language. Nobody wants to seem pretentious, or almost nobody. Why then do lawyers so often seem so? Pretentiousness must not be as easy to avoid as we think. Part of the problem is that "we" are never pretentious; "they" are. "I" am serious, "you" are formal, "he" is pretentious—which of course will not be his view of the matter at all. How can we come to see in ourselves the pretentiousness that others see in us?

Many of the words that strike readers as pretentious have come into English from Latin or Norman French, itself a Latinate language. In modern English, we often have a choice between a word of Latinate derivation and another of Germanic derivation. It is usually easy to hear the differences in connotation. *Before* seems less pretentious than *prior to*. A *will* is less portentous than a *testament* or a *will and testament*. *Beef* is more appetizing than *cow*. A *bloody* murder is more . . . well, bloody than a *sanguinary* one.

Lawyers can make their writing appear to be much more down-to-earth and straightforward by using what are sometimes called "good old Anglo-Saxon words." But such language can be faulted as "chatty," "colloquial," or even "slangy." Let's say you decide that *will* and *testament* mean the same thing: are you sure your client will think it's doing what it needs to do if you write only "My Will," instead of "Last Will and Testament?"

Lawyers faced with apparent synonyms may wonder whether there is a legal difference between one term and another. Lawyers may also consider it prudent not to "improve" the language of boilerplate provisions, or drafts of certain complicated agreements that are near to being consummated.

We began the account of the history of legal diction with the sentence "All languages are polyglot, and English is more polyglot than most." Instead of *polyglot*, which comes from the Greek, should we have used the word *mixed* because it is more familiar, less pretentious? Maybe. But *polyglot* in its root sense means "many tongued." *Mixed* doesn't have that connotation. We couldn't let it go.

There is no rule here that tells a writer what to do in all situations. Writers need to be aware of the options, and consider what the situation calls for. This is a book on effective legal writing, and if making writing "better" seems to decrease its chances of being effective, we do not recommend that the language be improved.

We need to realize, however, that simply repeating language that seems to have worked in some other situation can be a mask for incompetence. It makes the language of the law a mere formalism, rather than an instrument of meaning and communication. It's a practice that may save time in the short run but cause real problems later.

Here a list of some Latinate words and Germanic English equivalents

Latinate	Germanic English
attorney	*lawyer*
purchase	*buy*
request	*ask*
devise	*bequeath*
infant	*child*
larceny	*theft*
marriage	*wedding*
property	*goods*
pledge	*borrow*

How to Avoid Ineffective Legalese. Critics of the diction of lawyers concentrate their disdain on *legalisms*—the expressions that make lawyers sound like lawyers. If the concern is effective writing, it is misleading to think that it is always better to avoid sounding like a lawyer. There are times when "plain English" is what is effective and times when it is not.

A great many of the expressions the public associates with lawyers contribute nothing to precision and certainty of meaning: they are used only because they sound "legal."

> *said*
> *herein, hereinbefore, hereinabove, hereinunder,*
> *hereinafter*
> *prior to, subsequent to, concomitantly with*

> You present a title attorney with a deed that says the title is "clear," and are asked "Why don't you say 'free and clear?' Everybody else does." It is easier to comply than to explain.
>
> —A senior lawyer

therein
such
said
aforesaid
respectively

Legalese of this sort is used in all sorts of situations where it is pointless and even off-putting to the recipient. Lawyers who think it creates greater precision are kidding themselves. But in some situations—will, trusts, some contracts—it can enhance client satisfaction.

Numerals. The earliest scriveners, plying their art with goose quills, penknives, and ink from the glands of squid, and engaged in writing documents directed to a largely illiterate audience, had reason to write numbers in words *and* figures thus: "six (6) acres." Their successors followed the practice, using steel nib pens and parchment. One would have thought that Roman numerals would have been preferred, since they would have been easier than Arabic numbers to write with a balky goose quill.

The practice survives, even though since the advent of the typewriter, it has become unnecessary. Secretaries feel they have become "legal" secretaries the first time they use words and figures in a document. Exhaustive research into legal secretaries' desk manuals fails to reveal any mandate to clutter up a text with words and figures. It's doubtful that writing numbers in both words and figures does much to increase a client's sense of security.

At least we've been spared "six (VI) acres." Nobody recommends the use of Roman numbers. They are all right for outlines, but they divert attention when, in the higher denominations, the reader has to stop and start counting fingers (how much is MCVIII?). Anything that diverts the reader's attention is ineffective legal writing.

How to Avoid Ineffective Jargon. Lawyers are also urged to avoid *jargon.* But the proper use of jargon is essential to effective legal writing. Every profession, every identifiable social group, has a jargon—a language that means some-

---

A veteran judge from Arkansas once asked a group of judges at a writing seminar if they would say: "Dear, that is the best apple pie you've ever made. May I have another piece of said pie?"

What do you do if the two numbers aren't the same because one got changed and the other didn't during editing? All you can do is get into a swearing contest. I've seen this happen twice.

—A partner

Judge to lawyer who had number paragraphs with Roman numerals: "If you think Roman numerals are so great, send your clients their bills in Roman numerals!"

thing different to the members of the group than it does to nonmembers. For a lawyer, the question is not whether to use this special language, but when, how, and with whom.

Beginning law students may use this special language primarily to proclaim their desire for membership in the group. If their jargon were translated into plain English, all that would be lost would be the pretentious tone.

But that isn't always all that is lost when jargon is translated into plain English. Legal terms of art, for the people who understand them, do not simply refer to concepts that can be translated into plainer language. Law school teaches us how these terms raise questions and issues that can ramify indefinitely. For a lawyer, *negligence* carries meanings that *fault* does not.

Jargon is also necessary to effectiveness when it appears in the language of IRS regulations that lawyers writing wills and trusts will depart from at their peril.

For readers in some situations, the complexity that a term carries for a lawyer may be expendable, even counterproductive. The holder of an automobile insurance policy may need to know what to say and what not to say after a car accident. In such a case, lawyers should talk about "fault" than about "negligence," even though the question of "negligence" is what a jury may finally be called upon to decide.

Certain words which may appear to be pretentious jargon, like *fungible, ductile,* and *miscible,* define precisely a condition or process in one word, saving the time of both writer and reader, if the reader knows what the word means. It takes Black's Law Dictionary twenty-nine words to express the same idea as *fungible.* The definition for *ductile* is ten words long. Precise such terms may be, but if your reader is likely to be befuddled or put off by them, it may be best to translate them with some "extra" words. The dictionary's definition may or may not be helpful here. Dictionary definitions may use jargon to define jargon. You may have to develop your own definition in language appropriate for your reader.

> **Should we have said that *negligence* carries a *penumbra* of meaning that *fault* does not? We wrote that at first, but after a good editor who is not a lawyer questioned it, we decided that this Latinate term added nothing to our purpose, despite its common occurrence in legal discourse**

How to Avoid Sexist Language. Many states have statutes or case law providing that words of the masculine gender include the feminine and vice versa. In these states, reliance on one or the other gender in writing would have no effect in law. But effective legal writing concerns itself with more than legal effect. Effective legal writing does not offend its intended readers. Today many of a lawyer's intended readers are offended by sexist usages, and many of these readers are men.

In some situations still, sexist usages may be effective. Some readers might be moved in the way you want by a reference to "the weaker sex," or "the little woman." Ethical considerations aside, legal writers must realize that words that are written down often end up being read by audiences other than those for whom they were immediately intended. As a legal writer, it would be short-sighted and unwise to rely on sexist language to accomplish your goal.

In the last few decades, we have become more aware of how often "normal" ways of speaking exclude the feminine gender. The President of the United States not long ago characterized his nominee to the United States Supreme Court "the best man for the job." The co-president of a women's rights organization suggested that he might have said the best *person* for the job.

Because sexist usages are embedded in the culture, we cannot simply decide to avoid them and be done with it. They spring "naturally" to mind. They find their way into our drafts in spite of our intentions. We catch them (though perhaps not all of them) only when we revise. As time goes by, we will be less likely to produce them. But this is a challenge that must be addressed, like many in writing, one draft at a time.

The solutions to problems of sexist usage in language are not always obvious. It can require some dexterity to accomplish nonsexist usages without distracting readers with phrasing that seems unconventional. By careful revision, we can avoid the constructions that some regard as unhappy solecisms: him/her, her/him, s/he, her or him, him or her. We might want to use just such a conspicuous construction in some situations, however, to draw attention to the fact that women are being included where before they had been excluded.

Here are some of the sexist usages we revised out of this book. Notice that we often took the opportunity to revise more that the sexist usage, to make the sentence more clear or emphatic.

These are the means by which you learn what the other fellow [side] is up to

***

The witness in an oral deposition can refresh his memory.

Witnesses . . . can refresh their memories.

***

With the material gained from the opposing party, you can pin him down.

Opposing parties can be pinned down . . . .

***

It is far better to state the facts, and allow the judge to arrive, on his or her own, at the conclusion that your opponent is at fault.

It is far better to state the facts, and allow judges to arrive, on their own, at the conclusion that your opponent is at fault.

***

The losing lawyer will be interested in the reasons for judgment, not, of course, because he wants to learn how it is that his client should have lost the case, but to see if there are grounds for appeal.

Losers will then be interested in the reasons for judgment, not, of course, to learn how it is that their clients should have lost, but to see if there are grounds for appeal.

***

He who seeks equity must do equity.

Those who seek equity must do equity.

Should lawyers flag sexist language in material they are quoting with a [sic] or a notation like "[sexist language in original]"? Not if they are offering the quotation as support for their position. To undermine it in one way might invite the reader to undermine it in another. In most cases, it will be obvious to a reader that you are simply quoting accurately the sexist language of the original. Even if you want to undermine the argument of the quotation, challenging its sexist language might distract the reader from the primary basis for our challenge and might be seen as overreaching.

Avoiding sexism is not just a matter of watching your pronouns. What if we had written in the section on Writing through the Trial "Lawyers should act like boxers who are able to shake hands after the bout"? This comparison might be said to exclude women (though boxing matches between women are staged today). Now what if the sentence is rewritten to "Lawyers should act like the athletes who are able to shake hands with their opponents after the contest"? At one time, this might also have been said to exclude women. But since athletes who are women have recently become much more prominent in popular culture, it no longer excludes them, and the assumption that it does could itself be seen as sexist.

Here are some terms that will allow you to avoid the generic use of "man" to refer to adults of both sexes.

Instead of	Consider
mankind	*humanity, human beings, people*
man's achievements,	*human achievements*
best man for the job	*best person, best man or woman*
man-made	*synthetic, manufactured, crafted, machine-made*
the common man	*ordinary people*

Notice that the preferred alternatives are often more abstract that what they are offered to replace, and sometimes longer, harder to pronounce. The sexist examples can seem more "natural," more vivid. This simply points up how when we commit ourselves to avoiding sexist language, we may not be able to find an alternative that is preferable on all counts to the language we wish to replace.

When referring to the holders of particular jobs

Instead of	Consider
chairman	*coordinator (of committee or department), moderator (of a meeting), presiding officer, head, chair*
businessman	*business executive or manager*
fireman, mailman	*fire fighter, mail carrier*
policeman & -woman	*police officer*

Notice that nonsexist usages are not always more abstract. "Chair" is in fact shorter and punchier than "chairman."

To avoid the masculine (or feminine) singular pronoun following the use of a noun (*the judge . . . he, the attorney . . . he, the secretary . . . she*), you can recast into the plural.

Instead of	Consider
Give each client his due	*Give clients their due*

You can replace the masculine or feminine pronoun with one, you, or (sparingly) he or she, as appropriate. Finally, you can alternate male and female examples and expressions.

With indefinite pronouns (*everybody, everyone, anybody, anyone*), the plural pronoun (*their*) has become an acceptable substitute for the masculine singular pronoun in all but strictly formal usage.

Instead of	Consider
Anyone who wants to write effectively should watch his diction.	*Anyone who wants to write effectively should watch their diction.*

This nonsexist usage violates a convention of correct usage, since a plural pronoun (their) is used with a singular subject (anyone). When the legal writing calls for "strictly formal usage," as it almost always does, this option might not be desirable. A second revision might produce

> *Those who want to write effectively should watch their diction.*

Rewrite to Avoid Wordiness. Condense your references when possible. *The escrow agreement that was part of the transaction in which house was conveyed to Mrs. Jones* can be referred to in the next sentence as "*This agreement . . .*" and later as "*the agreement*," or, if it needs to be distinguished from other agreements, as "*the escrow agreement.*" There is no chance that the reader will be confused if we fail to repeat the full description. Legal writers often provide in parentheses an abbreviation or summary term ("the agreement"). This is sheer legalism most of the time. It does nothing to help the reader stay on track.

At the level of diction, an especially mindless form of wordiness appears in expressions like

> *future plans,*

preplanned,

advance prediction,

visual observation,

a free complimentary copy.

completely surrounded on all sides.

The last term in the list adds wordiness to wordiness.

Mindlessness also appears in the wordy expressions that, because we hear them so often, readily roll out on to our pages:

Rather than	Prefer
due to the fact that	*because*
The question as to whether or not	*whether*
This is an argument which...	*This argument*

> Judge Smith claimed he had never seen the word respectively used except where no one but an idiot could have gotten the references wrong.
>
> —A writing consultant

Effective and Ineffective Platitudes. Lawyers do not want to write in ways that call attention to their own originality with language. The reader may enjoy your writing "burning my books behind me" (as E. B. White wrote in his essay on Will Strunk) instead of the platitudinous "burning my bridges behind me." But if the reader is distracted from your persuasive purpose, you have made your writing less, not more effective.

> Professor Strunk—so says his student E.B. White—responded to the expression "'the fact that'" with a quiver of revulsion and wrote that it should be "'revised out of every sentence in which it occurs.'" "But," says E. B. White, "a shadow of gloom seems to hang over the page, and you feel that he knows how hopeless his cause is. I suppose I have written 'the fact that' a thousand times in the heat of composition, revised it out maybe five hundred times in the cool aftermath. To be batting only .500 this late in the season, to fail half the time to connect with this fat pitch, saddens me, for it seems a betrayal of the man who showed me how to swing at it and made the swinging seem worthwhile."
>
> — E. B. White, "Will Strunk," *The Points of My Compass,* New York: Harper Collins, 1957, 1962.

Webster defines a *platitude* as a "dull, stale or insipid truism." Not even lawyers wish to be "dull, stale or insipid." They may want a statement to be taken as a *truism,* however, which Webster defines as "a statement of truth that is obvious and well known." Platitudes are deeply embedded in the

English and American common law systems. In the practice of law in these systems, platitudes can be your friends. The "rules" of common law arise inductively, from a number of cases being decided the same way. These rules operate not like the rules of the civil codes, but like the "rules" that one finds in proverbs.

Early on in the history of the common law, lawyers would quote proverbs to judges to advance their arguments. Many proverbs can be directly contradicted by other proverbs, of course—"Haste makes waste" is countered by "He who hesitates is lost," for example. Proverbs can rise to the level of "maxims," which are, as the classical rhetoricians knew, an effective tool in argument, even if they are platitudinous.

In the law of equity, maxims are particularly important. Some of these:

> *Equity aids the diligent (and the vigilant).*

> *Those who seek equity must do equity.*

> *An equity which is prior in time is better in right.*

> *Equity will not suffer a wrong to be without a remedy.*

> *Equity regards as done that which ought to have been done.*

> *Equity regards substance and intent, rather than form.*

Platitudinous though they may be, such maxims offer effective ways of making your case.

Platitudes work against effectiveness when they suggest a lazy use of language.

Effective Writing

Effective and Ineffective Boilerplate. Boilerplate is language—often pretentious, jargon-ridden, legalistic language—that is not so much written as imported into legal documents. The advent of electronic data banks and word processors make it much easier to import such language.

Boilerplate becomes boilerplate because it is familiar to lawyers or because it has been interpreted by a court. It was interpreted by a court because it wasn't clear in the first place. After it is interpreted, it is more clear in its legal effect—to some lawyers and judges at least—than is language that would be easier to understand. The monster begins to reproduce itself.

Lawyers will sometimes import boilerplate provisions into drafts of contracts for no better reason than that they found it in the form book or the firm's data bank. When this prolongs the process of negotiation and review, it does a disservice to the client.

But in some situations—wills, trusts, some contracts—lawyers will "improve" the language of certain boilerplate provisions at their peril. Regulations of the IRS may call for certain language to be used and none other, language that will be intelligible only to the specialist.

In deciding whether to use boilerplate, assess honestly your knowledge of the law in the area, assess your duty to your client, and finally assess your duty to the language, which includes the duty not to deploy mindlessly the turgid language of much boilerplate. Then do what needs to be done.

Find the Exact Word. Effective legal writers will understand that, as Mark Twain is reported to have said, "The difference between the right word and the word that is almost right is like the difference between lightning and the lightning bug." Effective legal writers will care about the difference between

> *uninterested* (apathetic) and *disinterested* (not having an interest in the outcome and thus more likely to be impartial)

> a *parameter* (a fixed value) and a *perimeter* (a

The judge lectured the young lawyers before him. "I don't want you using *contact* when you mean *communicated with*. The root for *contact* is the root for *touch*. And I don't want you to use *indicate* when you mean *said*. The root for *indicate* is the root for *point*. Understood?"

"Yes, your honor."

"Very well. Are you ready to proceed?"

"Your honor, when I contacted my client about this matter, she indicated she would need more time."

161

circular boundary)

flout and *flaunt*

flagrant and *blatant*

construction and *interpretation*

misfeasance and *malfeasance.*

They will find significant the etymologies of words, like

contact, which suggests *touching,*

indicate, which suggests *pointing out,*

arrive, which suggests *coming to shore.*

They will use words in ways that respect their histories.

Lawyers are not language scholars. They won't know all there is to know about English etymology. But they recognize the contribution such knowledge can make to effective writing, and they will use the dictionary for more than checking spelling. Some will actually enjoy learning what dictionaries can teach us about the lives of words.

Rewrite for Effective Citation and Quotation

Lawyers are bound by precedent and must reason about the present from the past. Most of the time, they don't want to appear original. They want their voice to join a chorus that is already singing. They accomplish this by citing and quoting authority, but many lawyers do not do this effectively.

Cite pertinently rather than scholastically. In citation, more is not better. Long strings of citations are common in today's legal writing. Lawyers may have imported this practice from their experience working on the law review, or reading appellate opinions. The practice suggests that authority for a proposition is created by a process of saturation rather than by appropriately applied precedent.

If your reader is sophisticated, as judges are, the appearance of a long string of citations can have an untoward effect. Sophisticated readers sense that more is less in this case. They know that the Air Force drops lots of bombs when it isn't sure it can hit what it is aiming at. They know that if you had a good case for your purpose, you would use it. When you don't have a case that is determinative, and you often won't, you should still select judiciously and cite only those cases from which you will quote something.

Judges don't like to be lectured on the law. Nor are judges likely to be impressed by your scholarly attainments. They have a case to decide.

If a case is worth citing, it is worth quoting. If you follow this maxim, you will cite fewer cases than many lawyers do, far fewer than do writers who have imported the practices of law review writing into the practice of law. Your use of authority will be more effective, however.

If a number of authorities can be quoted to support a point, quote them—briefly, pertinently.

It is possible to quote too much. Lawyers want other voices helping them, but they don't want those voices distracting the reader from the particular business at hand. The judge needs to decide the case at bar, not to learn everything there may be to know about a particular legal point.

Quote rather than paraphrase. The difference between quotation and paraphrase is the difference between lightning and lightning bug, to paraphrase Mark Twain. Never paraphrase what you can quote. Paraphrase, which puts someone else's language in your own words, can be useful to introduce a quotation. It allows you to condense verbiage that neither you nor your reader needs. But paraphrase adds your interpretation to the language. The court wants the cited court's authority, not yours. If you force the judge to go to the library to check the citation, and the judge concludes that the language doesn't say what you say it does, you are in serious trouble.

Paraphrase allows you to make analogies, which is what we used it for at the beginning of this section. Twain did not say exactly what we wanted to say (he was talking about the difference between the right word and the word that is almost right), so we got something from him through paraphrase. Think how much more powerfully he would have contributed to our argument if we had been able to quote him to support directly the point we wanted to make.

Quotations should be short and pertinent. Lawyers and judges often quote from authorities as if quotations were rocks deployed to secure a flapping tent in a high wind. Great chunks of quotation are inserted into documents, the heavier the better. As we have said, when readers encounter a large block of language, they skip it. They hope that the writer will point out the pertinent part of the quotation later in the discussion. Readers know they can return to the block, if need be, when they have learned just what they need to be looking for in it. Let the reader know, going into the quotation, the pertinence of the language you are about to quote.

Lawyers and judges tend to introduce quotations with unhelpful phrases like "Section I of the Uniform Commercial Code reads. . . ." perhaps adding, hopefully, ". . . in pertinent part . . ."—a gesture that acknowledges a reader's needs but doesn't do anything to address them. It asserts that the language is pertinent but it doesn't explain how. Avoid non-introductions that just announce the quotation or tell where it came from, without also revealing the pertinence of the quotation.

Don't lead into your quotations with the detailed citation. Lead sentences should be making your arguments. Do not write

> *Section 288 (c) iii 4, of the Revised Statutes of Ontario as amended, says . . ."*

when you could write

> *Fraudulent sales are unenforceable, under Ontario Statutes, when . . .*

Provide the full citation at the end.

To impress upon your readers the authority of the language you are about to quote, you may want to tell them the source of the quotation going in—for example, that the statute you are about to quote from is part of the Uniform

Commercial Code, or the case you are about to quote from was decided by a court in the same federal circuit. But do not distract your reader with the detailed citation: put that at the end of the introductory material, or the end of the quotation.

To make your quotations pertinent, you need to do more than tell your reader the source of a quotation. You need to tell them how the information relates to your argument: "Section 1 of the Uniform Commercial Code recognizes the appropriateness of estoppel in cases like this one," or "In Michigan, estoppel was held to be appropriate in cases like this one." You show the reader the pertinence of the quotation by stating its relationship to the issue being discussed.

Don't just import a quotation. Judges can and do spot the lazy writers who simply import quotations. Word processors, formbank software, and computerized research programs now allow us to import great chunks of quotation into our documents at no cost to us or our staff in time or effort. Writers concerned about effectiveness, however, will employ not just the *research* technology offered by the data bases but also the *revision* technology offered by word processing. They will do more than "assemble" their documents.

Some rewriting works better when you do it on paper, including rewriting to select the pertinent language to quote and to integrate it forcefully into the argument. Once you have made the changes on paper, word processors can quickly make the changes you want in your draft.

Don't quote more than five lines. If you do, the approved way is to indent and single space the material, without using quotation marks at the beginning and end. Do not be afraid to set apart shorter quotations in this manner if it is material you want especially to emphasize. You can usually find the pertinent language in what you have underlined in the block of quoted language you were about to dump into your draft.

Be absolutely accurate in quotation and citation. Accuracy is the sine qua non of effective citation and quotation. A faulty citation infects your whole argument. Law schools teach the conventions of correct citation to authority. These conventions, found in the Blue Book, have been well established in the United States. Some variations on Blue Book practice are being proposed in some areas, but observing Blue Book conventions is still part of accurate citation.

When you quote, you are telling your readers that they can rely on the absolute accuracy of the language you quote. Even typographical errors will seriously damage your credibility with a judge. The judge may have been thinking of adopting the quoted language. A greater sin is to quote out of context, and it is stupid to try to mislead the court in this way. Never try to mislead the court about the import of the language you are quoting. That's always fatal.

When the material you want to quote itself carries mistakes of spelling or mechanics, or diction you do not want to adopt as your own (sexist or racist language, for example), you can let the reader know this with "[sic]," which is Latin for "thus." It tells the reader that the objectionable language in the quoted material is not yours. If you want your quotation to speak for you, it is best to find material that does not need to be "corrected" in this way.

If you find any errors in the quotations of your opponents, be sure to point them out to the judge. Do this in a matter-of-fact way, not accusingly. These mistakes make your opponent's quotations considerably less effective, especially if your opponent hasn't noticed them.

Brackets [ ] can be used to insert explanatory material into quoted language, or to substitute diction you prefer for the diction you object to in quoted material. Brackets can also be used to allow you to interpolate comments in a quotation, a practice that may help keep the reader on track. But it is best not to interpolate in quotations that are authority for your propositions. The court will not adopt language with bracketed interpolations in it.

You can and should use ellipsis points (. . .) to tell the judge that you have left language out of a quotation when it is not otherwise obvious. But note that using a quotation with an ellipsis in it might send the judge or the judge's staff straight to the library to see what you left out and why.

Integrate quoted material. If you can integrate the quoted material into the flow of your own sentences, your argument will read more convincingly. This makes "your" argument appear to be an argument that is supported in the positions of others. If your first draft says

> Section 25-381.18 states who can begin annulment proceedings:
>
> *If, however, after the expiration of such period, the controversy between the spouses has not been terminated, either spouse may institute proceedings for annulment of marriage. . . .*

rewrite as

> *Annulment proceedings can be instituted by "either spouse." 25-381.18.*

Don't use footnotes. In legal writing, except for the scholarly kind, footnotes almost always diminish effectiveness.

Footnotes and the scholarly apparatus they create have been ridiculed since Cervantes. They persist. They remain *de rigueur* in the law review article, but they have recently been called into question in another bastion of footnote-ery by a justice of the United States Supreme Court. If your reader is likely to take numerous footnotes as *ipso facto* a sign of scholarly attainment, and if scholarly attainment is what you need to demonstrate to your reader, then footnotes are recommended. So, *mutatis mutandis*, is the use of Latin phrases like *ipso facto* and *mutatis mutandis*. Evidence of scholarly attainment is not what makes writing effective in the practice of law.

Footnotes are sometimes promoted as a way of increasing readability by not interrupting the reader. But attentive readers know they need to take the time to read the footnotes when they encounter them in a text. It's often in the footnotes that scholars—and lawyers and judges—acknowledge problems with their argument that are inconvenient to acknowledge in the text.

> **This case involves candles.[1]**
> **[1] Candles have been known since antiquity.**
> —A judge, with tongue-in-cheek

Footnotes can be a convenient place for lawyers to dump string citations that they may have been told they should not have in their written arguments. This won't increase effectiveness, but your reader will thank you.

Checklist: Guidelines for Effective Citation and Quotation

- Cite pertinently rather than scholastically.

- If a case is worth citing, it is worth quoting.

- Quote rather than paraphrase.

- Quotations should be short and pertinent.

- Do not lead into your quotations with the detailed citation information.

- Don't just import a quotation.

- Don't quote more than five lines.

- Be absolutely accurate in quotation and citation.

- Integrate quoted material.

- Don't use footnotes.

Proofread

Spell Correctly. Correct spelling is important because apparent carelessness in spelling allows the reader to infer carelessness in other areas. Writing that strikes a reader as careless will not be effective.

Some spelling errors are more harmful to effectiveness than others. It isn't at all helpful to misspell the name of the judge, or the name of the party you are negotiating with. It is not quite so harmful to spell *judgment* as *judgement*. If your readers notice the mistake—and not all will—they may allow that it is a "natural" mistake, or they may suspect that you spent some time in Britain, where the North

American spelling is the "wrong" one. Nonetheless, in North America, it's *judgment*.

It is lawyerly to pronounce the word *defendant* as "defend*ant*." The practice may have started because until we accent that syllable we aren't sure what the correct vowel is. Unaccented syllables are trouble spots for spelling (Capit*a*l? Capit*o*l? Rep*i*tition? Rep*e*tition?) because the sound of the spoken word gives no clue as to the letter. Notice that in third syllable of *repetition*, which is accented, there is no question about the correct vowel. Writers can sometimes figure out which vowel is correct by finding a form of the word that accents the syllable with the vowel in question.

How to Check Spelling. Word processors come with programs that check spelling. They are helpful in catching common spelling mistakes like getting the vowel wrong in unaccented syllables. Spell checkers will not catch all mistakes, however, and many they don't catch are of the more harmful kind.

- They will stop you at the name of the judge, as they will at other proper names, but won't tell you if you spelled the name wrong.

- They won't tell you that you confused *capital* with *capitol* or *their* with *there* or *they're*.

- They won't tell you that you put an apostrophe in *its* when you shouldn't have (though they will if you put one in *yours* or *theirs*).

- They won't tell you that you wrote *principal* when you should have written *principle*, or *affect* when you should have written *effect*. Or *parameter* when you should have written *perimeter*. Or *prior to* when you should have written *before*.

- They won't tell you that your indefinite pronouns (*it, they, these*) don't have a clear reference in what precedes them.

- They may not tell you that you mismatched the number of a noun and verb ("The members of the committee

. . . is. . . ." This kind of mistake is more likely to be made if the subject is separated from the verb by a long string of other words.

- They won't catch many typos—if you type *if* instead of *is*, for example, or *now* instead of *not*, or *none* instead of *one*, just to mention a few typos that could make a big difference.

Always proofread in hard copy. Do not rely only on your spell checker, or your secretary, to correct spelling. You are the one who must stand behind the product.

How to Punctuate Effectively

Effective punctuation can sometimes be a matter of punctuating, consciously, in ways that are not conventional. More often, conventional punctuation is required in effective legal writing because it doesn't distract the reader.

Punctuation can affect the tone, not just the correctness, of your writing. Punctuation signals readers what to do with their voices The appropriate tone is crucial to effectiveness.

Commas and Periods. When the goal is effective writing, it is important to recognize that punctuation gives readers signals about where to pause and how to inflect their voices. The period was originally used, in medieval manuscripts, to indicate where someone reading the manuscript aloud should pause for breath. Today we say "Periods should be placed at the end of sentences." The end of a sentence, however, is a place where the voice of a reader will be inflected in a distinctive way. The comma calls for a different kind of pause and inflection, one that is less conclusive. If you read this sentence aloud, you'll be able to hear the difference between the pauses and inflections after the word *voice* and *sentence*, and the one here at the end of the sentence.

Writers who use commas where a period is called for (producing what writing teachers call a "run-on sentence") recognize that they want the reader to pause at that point, but they signal a partial pause rather than the conclusive one.

More common in legal writing is the use of commas where none is needed. When we read a sentence aloud, or hear it in our mind's ear, we pause more often than necessary. Sometimes we drop commas into those places. Here is a test: if you can read a string of words, through a place where you have called for a pause with a comma, without pausing, and without confusing your reader, delete the comma. The first three commas should be deleted in the preceding sentence.

Commas (and the vocal inflection they call for) can affect meaning in ways that can make a big difference to a lawyer. Above we wrote "The period was originally used, in medieval manuscripts, to indicate where someone reading the manuscript aloud should pause for breath." The commas told the reader to pause after "used" and "manuscripts," and those pauses told the reader that we meant that in medieval manuscripts the period was used for a certain purpose, not that the period was first used in medieval manuscripts. Grammarians refer to this as the difference between "restrictive" and "nonrestrictive" clauses. Restrictive clauses call for commas. Nonrestrictive ones do not. It makes a difference to meaning, not just form.

Most writers who misuse periods and commas seem to do so either because they are trying to follow a vaguely understood rule, or else because they are not being careful enough about what the voice would be doing at a particular place if the language were being read aloud. When we hear a sentence read aloud, we know whether a phrase is being used restrictively or non-restrictively. If we don't know and need to find out, we can ask the person who uttered the words. Readers can't ask this question of the documents they are reading. Writers need to get this one right on their own or with an editor's help.

The Apostrophe. The apostrophe has two conventional uses:

- to tell the reader that a *word's* had some letters left out (In *word's*, the first two letters in the word *has* are left out), or

- to create a possessive noun and to tell the reader whether a *noun's number* is singular or plural (Here *number* belongs to *noun*. We know also that it is one noun not many because of the article *a*. But what if we see *the partners assets*? With the apostrophe after the *r*, one partner's assets is being referred to. With it after the *s*, we are referring to the assets of more than one partner. Obviously, this could make a big difference to the effect of a legal document.

Writers in English commonly use *it's* incorrectly. Notice that *it's* is a contraction (a word with an apostrophe to show that letters have been left out). It's short for *it is*. It is not the possessive form of the pronoun *it*. *Its* is a possessive pronoun all by itself. It's easy when drafting to put the apostrophe in when you don't want it: your spell checker will not catch this one.

Notice also that a contraction has a less formal, even chatty quality, as you can see just above and in the first sentence of this section. If chattiness is what you want, contractions can help. Chattiness is not effective in most legal writing.

Exclamation Points (with observations on *Really* and *Very*). Exclamation points are used by novice writers to emphasize a point or express sincere conviction. In legal writing exclamation points may well communicate a lack of substance.

Compare

> *If you don't pay up, I'll sue. I really mean it!*

with

> *Please pay by tomorrow at 4:45. If payment has not been received by that time, the complaint we have prepared (draft enclosed) will be on the way to the courthouse.*

The adverbs "really" and "very" have the same unhappy effect in legal writing. Consider the first example just above: Would adding another "really" decrease or increase the reader's sense that the writer "meant it"?

"Very" is often used in an effort to intensify something that cannot be intensified. *Unique* means "one of a kind." *Very unique* doesn't make something more unique: it makes it less so, since it appears you don't know what the word means. What about *very negligent?* Or *very guilty?* Negligence and guilt are either-or logical categories, like zero or one. While we are not likely to be misunderstood if we use such expressions, the usage is sloppy and can make our language less effective. You can't be "very pregnant," or "not very pregnant," either. When we refer to some people as "very pregnant," the reference is not to the state of being either pregnant or not, but to the expectant mother's size, or readiness to deliver. It's a colorful usage not likely to be useful in formal legal writing.

Colons and Dashes. Colons and dashes are used to let readers know that the writer is about to go on and develop the statement just made: several kinds of development may ensue: an explanation, a summary, a series, a quotation: or a kicker of some other kind: such as in:

> *It's easy when drafting to put the apostrophe in its when you don't want it: your spell checker will not catch this one.*

Use colons only at the ends of independent clauses, not at the ends of phrases. Don't use too many colons or dashes. This creates clutter. Don't use "such as" to lead into a colon: that's just what the colon implies. These rules are all violated in the introductory paragraph above. A better version would be

> *Colons and dashes are used to let readers know that the writer is about to go on and develop the statement just made. Several kinds of development may ensue: an explanation, a summary, a series, a quotation, or a kicker of some other kind.*

Dashes can be used like colons. They have a less formal, somewhat more dramatic quality than colons. Young writers tend to use them a lot (along with exclamation points). They can give a kind of breathless quality to prose.

Dashes can be used when you want to interrupt yourself—though in legal writing it's not often you want appear to do that—and can be used (like parentheses) in the middle of a sentence, while colons should be used only at the ends of independent clauses.

Parentheses. When we are thinking hard about complex matters as we write (lawyers often are) we are likely to interrupt ourselves with new thoughts (like the need for examples for the reader) which we can insert into sentences using parentheses (not to be confused with dashes). We can also use commas or dashes. Parentheses are more emphatic than commas.

Usually it is better to revise parenthesis-riddled prose not merely by replacing parentheses with commas or dashes but by reordering the elements of the sentence or paragraph. The first sentence of this section might become

> *Lawyers often have to think about complex matters as they write. Parentheses can be used to insert new thoughts into sentences and to provide examples for the reader.*

Lawyers and academics tend to overqualify when they write. Ranks of parentheses can be a sign of this.

Quotation Marks. Effective legal writers quote effectively (see pp. 162-168). To quote effectively, you must know how to punctuate quotations.

To begin with, be aware that quotation marks offer a very specific assurance to readers: they say that if readers go to the specific passage that has been cited, they will find the language to be *exactly* as the writer has rendered it. *The first requirement for effective quotation is absolute accuracy.* In a quotation, no typographical error is harmless. Any error calls into question the writer's ability to deliver on the assurance of absolute accuracy. It infects the whole undertaking. Inaccurate citation has an even worse effect, if possible.

To make quotations more effective, legal writers sometimes need to add something to it. More often they need to subtract distracting material from it. If you wish to *add* something to the quoted material that does not appear there, use brackets. In this way you can clarify references [Mrs. Johnson's employer], tell the reader that you have supplied emphasis [Emphasis supplied] or add other comments [Can you believe this?]. You cannot correct errors in the original. When you have errors in the original, you can reassure the reader about your own accuracy by adding [Errors in original] or by inserting [sic] after the mistake. *Sic* is Latin for *thus*.

If you wish to *delete* something from the middle of a quotation, you tell the reader you have done so with three ellipsis points (. . .). You should do this at the beginning of your quotation if it is not otherwise apparent that you left something out. If there are words at the end of a sentence beyond those you want to quote, you use the three ellipsis points and add a period.

C Checklist Inventory

Habits of Mind and Practice

- Notice effective writing.
- Get help from others on your writing.
- Recognize that writing is a powerful tool for thinking.
- Understand the importance of planning.
- Notice that legal writing, like other writing, has voice and communicates attitudes toward the reader.
- Understand that revision is crucial.

Facts

- Develop facts for yourself first chronologically and then revise them in order of importance as you develop your theory of the case.
- Distinguish *material* from merely *relevant* facts, and in arguing to judges, stick to the material facts.
- Before narrating facts to judges, let them know what the court is being asked to decide.
- Present the facts as a simple story, not as something that looks like a lawyer wrote it.
- Let the facts speak for themselves.
- Do not offer your opponent's version of the facts.
- Never fudge the facts.
- Do not fail to mention "bad" facts, but mention them in unemphatic ways.
- Argue the facts on every possible occasion—if they favor your client.

Forms

- Don't let forms cause you to underestimate the importance of the practice of fact.
- Consider the sources of forms.
- Compare different versions of forms.

- Don't assume any form covers all the bases.
- In forms that list many items, beware *exclusio unius.*
- Remember that using forms from a data bank can waste time if the document is to be reviewed and negotiated.
- Consider whether improvements to a familiar document will generate unnecessary alarm in the other side and prolong negotiation.
- Remember that printed forms are sometimes seen as more trustworthy.
- Revise printed forms through addenda, not interlineation.
- Remember that some clients will not appreciate having their special matter handled by a form.

Motions

- Am I making this motion in a good faith belief that it is valid?
- Does my motion begin with a statement of the nature of the case and the pertinent facts?
- Is this statement not more than 10 lines long?
- Does it contain all the material facts, while remaining concise?
- Does it state the matter dispassionately?
- If my motion argues a point of law
  Does it keep the argument to a narrow point?
  Does it avoid lecturing the judge?
  Are citations to the law and record absolutely accurate?
- Is the relief requested in language that the judge might adopt for the order?

Briefs on Appeal: Statement of the Facts

- Finish the statement of facts after you know precisely the argument you are going to make.
- Do not obviously argue the facts or color them.
- Do not overstate or fudge the facts.
- Tell the court the material facts, and perhaps a few facts that are merely relevant (if they help set the scene).
- Do not omit "bad" facts
- Do not quibble over trivial matters.
- Consider how you will refer to the parties.

Arguments

- Do not write as if you are simply out to "prove" your points.
- Provide a summary before the actual argument.
- Do not start your argument by repeating the argument of the other side.
- Don't list legal principles the court should know.
- Focus issues precisely on appeal.

- Try to understand your argument as a syllogism
- Consider carefully whether minor issues should be omitted.
- Be thorough but do not write exhaustive scholarly treatments of legal issues.
- Be absolutely accurate and complete in your use of authority.
- If a case is worth citing, it's worth quoting.
- Quote phrases, clauses, sentences.

Contracts: Particular Provisions

- Keep Certain Terms Flexible
- Do Not Use Terms That Produce Questions of Fact
- Specify Consideration
- Address the Possibility of Assignment
- Consider Whether to Provide for Attorney's Fees
- Consider Arbitration, Mediation, Alternative Dispute Resolution
- Be Careful With Provisions Calling for Forfeitures and Penalties

Summary: Brevity and Conciseness

- Concise thinking is necessary to effective writing whether the document is brief or long.
- We can often arrive at concise thinking more quickly by letting early writing take us there.
- Brevity and concise thinking are accomplished only through rewriting.
- To achieve brevity, write early, expecting to revise and select out what is necessary to your purpose and reader.
- Be brief when brevity would be effective.
- Brevity is usually preferred for one's peers.
- Decide what isn't necessary by referring to your purpose and intended reader.
- To achieve brevity, write early, expecting to revise and select only what is necessary to your purpose and reader.

Guidelines for Effective Citation and Quotation

- Cite pertinently rather than scholastically.
- If a case is worth citing, it is worth quoting.
- Quote rather than paraphrase.
- Quotations should be short and pertinent.
- Do not lead into your quotations with the detailed citation information.
- Don't just import a quotation. Integrate it.
- Don't quote more than five lines.
- Be absolutely accurate in quotation and citation.
- Don't use footnotes.

▐ Index of Topics